WRITING ENGLISH
A USER'S MANUAL

Nancy Harrison

CROOM HELM
London • Sydney • Dover, New Hampshire

© 1985 Nancy Harrison
Croom Helm Ltd, Provident House, Burrell Row,
Beckenham, Kent BR3 1AT
Croom Helm Australia Pty Ltd, First Floor,
139 King Street, Sydney, NSW 2001, Australia

British Library Cataloguing in Publication Data

Harrison, Nancy
    Writing English: A user's manual
    1. English language — Rhetoric
    I. Title
    808'.042   PE1408

    ISBN 0-7099-3708-3
    ISBN 0-7099-3709-1 Pbk

Croom Helm, 51 Washington Street, Dover,
New Hampshire 03820,USA

Library of Congress Cataloging in Publication Data

Harrison, Nancy.
    Writing English: A User's Manual

    (Croom Helm communication series)
    Includes index.
    1. English language — Grammar — 1950-
2. English language — Rhetoric. I. Title.
II. Series.
PE1112.H295   1985   808'.042   84-23144
ISBN 0-7099-3708-3
ISBN 0-7099-3709-1(pbk.)

Printed and bound in Great Britain
by Billing & Sons Limited, Worcester.

Contents

Acknowledgements

I am grateful to the following for permission to use copyright matter:

to The Society of Authors for a passage from *Fountains in the Sand* by the late Norman Douglas;

to W.H. Freeman Limited for sentences from *Enzyme Structure and Metabolism* by Dr Alan Fersht;

to Messrs Routledge and Kegan Paul for a passage from *Animal Senses* by Dr Maurice Burton;

to David Higham Limited for two short passages from *England Have My Bones* by the late T.H. White;

to Curtis Brown Limited for a passage from *He Died Old: Mithradates Eupator, King of Pontus* by the late Alfred Duggan;

and I wish to thank Edwin Guyton for sampling the material and making useful comments, and Dr Hills for a masterly display of patience and forbearance.

Preface

THE CROOM HELM COMMUNICATION SERIES

We are at the beginning of a communications revolution.

Developments in computers, electronic equipment and telecommunications are bringing information technology to all aspects of work and leisure.

These developments are focusing our attention on the storage, retrieval and use of information, the way we communicate with others, with ourselves, and with the world.

This series is intended to explore the many facets of communication from those concerned with developments in information technology to those concerned with other aspects of human communications.

This book provides a clear introduction to the use of written English. The author, Nancy Harrison, has many years of experience as a writer and editor. It is intended as a guide for anyone, student or professional, who wishes to improve the quality and precision of his written work.

P.J. Hills
Cambridge

Introduction

Written communication is the result of a primitive instinct, the desire to leave messages about the place for another creature to interpret. Stags do it; lemurs do it; even sheep do it. The stag advertises his readiness to set up a household and take on the management of a collection of wives: Buy Me – I am the Best. Lemurs use a chin gland to declare the limits of their territory: Private Property – Trespassers etc. Leading sheep mark a trail for the rest of the herd with secretions from glands in their feet: This Way.

It is not surprising that the human animal should refine and improve the communication code. But elaboration creates difficulties: the code must be intelligible to the largest number of fellow creatures. If we only had to sniff a letter or book to understand the contents, how easy literacy would be. Unfortunately, what is to be read has to be written, and many people make heavy weather of the simple urge to tell someone else of something by writing it down.

The Users

No one, except a diarist, writes solely for his or her own satisfaction. It is implicit in the act of writing that one does it to communicate with someone else. This makes us all writers, from the person who scrawls declarations on the ceilings of railway carriages to the author of a textbook. Whatever you write, you must get it right. 'Save the Wale' on the motorway flyover is a message wasted because of a mis-spelling; 'Out of order – use disabled toilet', an instruction pinned to a cloakroom door, apparently requires people to use plumbing that does not work.

To establish the dimensions of this book, certain assumptions have to be made. The readers for whom it is intended will have a reasonable command of spoken English; they read without effort and can think and form concepts in English; and they have a subject to write about, whether it is one being studied or researched, a part of their income-earning occupation or one that they teach. They may be students, people engaged in commerce or industry, members of professions or scientists. A further assumption is that they are not always certain of their ability to express themselves clearly and effectively on paper.

If, at any time, you have to write something to your advantage – an examination answer, a report or a learned text – you must acquire a sensitive ear for good English. Don't regard good English as a sort of mould into which the language is forced or a set of rules from which the language has developed. Language came first and the rules have grown from it. Good English is no more and no less than the use of the language according to widely accepted custom so that it is understood by the greatest number of people. It follows that certain conventions are observed so that written work is as clear to any reader in the world as it is to those on the writer's own doorstep or to members of a specialized group to which the writer belongs. What you write, or are about to write, has to be measured in terms of how it fulfils that intention of clear expression.

How to Use the Book

It is neither practicable nor sensible to assume that any reader will sit down and read a book on written English from beginning to end. All well and good if they do, but it is more likely that they will want to use it as a combination of dictionary and text: a source to which they go for advice, reassurance or argument. A book on this subject must be addressed to people with varying degrees of competence and experience. It must also cater for a number of different needs: acquisition of basic skills, reminders of points forgotten and the necessity to put a fluent grasp of language to work more efficiently. As it is offputting, not to say insulting, to come across advice and explanation which, for your level of knowledge, seems too simplistic, it is only right to expect readers to skip about, to turn to what seems most relevant to their needs or just to use the index to find a single topic.

Reference
The indexes: There are two indexes. The first is a short
guide to the sections dealing with problems that often seem
to crop up. You will find it at the end of this introduction.
The second is the main index. You will see that each paragraph in the text is numbered; both indexes use these numbers for references. The entries in the main index are followed first by a paragraph number in bold type which takes
you to the detailed discussion of the topic. Any other numbers, in roman type, refer to paragraphs in which the topic
is mentioned.

The glossary: When any technical term describing a point
of grammar is introduced in the text, it is printed in bold
type; all words in bold type are defined in the glossary. The
term will also be explained where it occurs or in the relevant
part of Chapter Three, Four or Five. Familiarity with a term
never arrives after one brief introduction; definitions stay
with one longer after several encounters. Use the glossary as
a concise grammatical dictionary.

The appendixes: Appendix I describes some useful books,
with comments about their particular uses. Appendix II
lists idiomatic associations of words: verbs that lose their
meaning when given the wrong preposition, nouns and
verbs that take the gerund or infinitive and phrasal verbs.

The text
The study of written English depends on recognizing what is
wrong rather than absorbing dictation about what is right. A
writer must learn to spot bad habits, clumsy constructions,
misused words and garbled meanings. To do so requires an
understanding of **grammar** and **syntax**. Grammar, like any
other science, has technical terms to define functions and
constructions; these functions and constructions are discussed in detail in the text. It is easier to avoid making
mistakes if you not only know how a word acts but also
understand the category into which it falls.

Chapter One looks at the present state of written English and the reasons for that state. If your interest in written work is purely practical, you may wish to move on to the next or later chapters. Chapter Two deals, in a basic way, with the development of a systematic approach to composition. It is intended for students and people whose careers have not yet demanded written work up to a professional or academic standard. It may also help those who find that the need to put something on paper produces panic – a state of mind known to many of us.

Chapters Three, Four and Five describe the parts of speech and their functions, with examples of abuse and proper application, examining their use in sentence construction. These chapters are intended for everyone who was not taught English grammar, or had not the opportunity of learning Latin or a structured European language at school. They may also be useful to those who have forgotten what they learnt.

Chapter Six introduces the parts played by punctuation, vocabulary and imagery in making written work understandable. It also discusses the development of an individual style. Chapter Seven, the last, reminds the writer of the essential relationship between what is written and the reader for whom it is written.

A CONCISE INDEX OF PROBLEMS AND SOLUTIONS

Turn directly to the paragraph number shown if you feel that something is wrong but are not sure into which grammatical area you have strayed.

Chapter One
The state of the art

1.1 Why should educated people write badly? Or, to put it another way, why do they fail to write clearly? The tool used is, for many of us, our native tongue and we have been speaking it, cajoling and quarrelling in it, learning through it and using it daily for much of our lives. Because speech, through imitation, assimilation and correction, is conquered first, turning thoughts into words ceases to be a conscious act. It is like driving a car, when hands and feet jiggle about doing the right things without direct orders.

1.2 In theory, we should only need to write down what we say and the message would be transmitted intelligently. In practice there is a problem of proximity. Speech is full of elisions, pauses and repetitions; perception of meaning depends as much on intuitive recognition of pauses and physical clues as it does on the actual words used. The reader, separated from the communicator, can rely on none of these.

1.3 Living in a world with a grudging respect for literature, we are often led to believe that the ability to write lucid prose is an inborn talent, like the artist's 'magic' pencil, and cannot be acquired. Perhaps there are writers so gifted, but most achieve clarity of expression through long and painful processes: revision and self-criticism. The best work is the result of real effort.

1.4 Since the second World War, the formal teaching of grammar has been largely abandoned. Reasons for doing so range from the dull teaching methods of the past to theories that see English as either an over-structured or a structureless language; in either case it is now often considered to be too difficult a subject to teach, even to the infant native English-speaker. While the old teaching methods may have been dull, they nevertheless gave the reasonably attentive child some information. Nowadays most pupils have to extrapolate; their written syntax has been cantilevered out from speaking. They leave school equipped with a ballpoint pen, the notion that only the content of written English matters, however unintelligible it may be, and three false rules:

Do not split an infinitive;
Do not end a sentence with a preposition;
Do not begin more than one sentence with 'I'.

1.5 The old-fashioned and pedestrian teaching of grammar made the production of written work somewhat easier. It gave some understanding of comparatives and relatives and a little knowledge of sentence structure. But familiarity with the phrase book does not make anyone a fluent speaker of a foreign language, nor can one become a pianist just by reading books on notation and technique. It is also necessary to practise and learn through one's mistakes.

1.6 Words form not only the cloth of a text; they are also the needles and pins used to tailor it to fit its purpose. The words and constructions taken into English from different sources have influenced the syntax. They have also been adapted and changed by usage. This erosion conceals the fact that absolute relationships and constructions still exist, although very often the same spelling covers all aspects of a word. Nouns may have lost their case endings and retained only singular and plural forms, but the case is still there, underlying their use. The language can be seen as a resurrection pie of leftovers. While each wave of invasion and immigration added something new, making the language rich and flexible, it also made the production of a simple set of rules to regulate usage very difficult.

1.7 The real educational gain from the study of Latin was the understanding it gave of a visibly structured language. Unfortunately, the purpose of such a study – its application to the comprehension of English grammar and syntax – seems seldom to have been made apparent to pupils whose boredom made them label it 'useless'. Agonizing as it was for lots of students, it had one advantage, a book of rules and precepts: the Latin grammar. Until the inflections and constructions became familiar, they could be checked against the book. It is a very practical way of working: reference to an authority, not once, but several times. The gain in confidence is worth the time.

1.8 It is not always convenient to rush to a rule book when the pen is poised over the paper, but convenience should give place to a desire for accuracy. The aim of every person who has to produce written work must be the acquisition of a feeling for what is right, a sense of correctness. If, when work is reread, there are hesitations and awkwardnesses, something must be wrong. It should have as natural a flow as a spontaneous conversation while being as precise in its meaning as a cornet solo. The rule book can help to identify areas of error and mistaken paths. Look on it as a combination of road map and guidebook.

False Trails
1.9 What goes wrong? If we can speak and read the language with ease, we ought to be able to express ourselve on paper. It seems that things go awry when subjects and verbs are mismatched; that sentences get out of hand and wind up in knots; that idiomatic usage is often not understood; and that inadequacies are often covered up with inappropriate terminology or high-flown language. To avoid these mistakes there must be an understanding, not only of the words in the language, but of the way in which they are fitted together for meaning.

1.10 Bad writing is not only a matter of syntactical errors, poor punctuation and mis-spelt words. A heavy hand with technical terms and elaborate constructions can produce a confusing text. The one who writes must always be aware of the one who reads. People who authorize projects or sign cheques are seldom scientists, researchers or engineers; more often they are administrators and are likely to prefer a simple explanation of how something works to a flood of professional jargon or language puffed up beyond the merits of its theme. They may well believe that a writer who cannot master lucid exposition has nothing worth saying.

1.11 No one is proof against the occasional silly mistake. Examination nerves are quite common and account for some blunders. Yet stress cannot explain the semi-literate writing of many students outside the examination room. A clue may be found in a book designed to coach pupils for O-level English Language and help them to revise the subject. The first section in the book deals with Summary Writing, evidently so important that it must be practised before reviewing grammar and syntax. Far from setting a good example, the section contains one long passage which is woefully ill-written. A disproportionate amount of the book is taken up with essay work, the meanings of proverbs and multiple choice questions. Only 30 of the 156 pages are devoted to grammar and sentence construction; much of the latter section is concerned, not with word-relationships, but with the meanings of words. Brief immutable (but often arguable) rules are given for usage with little explanation. If this book reflects the way in which examiners expect children to have been taught, the low standards are hardly surprising. Teaching that would emphasize the reasons behind accepted constructions, laying stress on conveying information, and training for a significant part of a child's educational life would enable a greater number of young people to express themselves fluently as a matter of course.

1.12 Some people distrust simplicity, choosing to hide behind catchphrases and jargon in case their utterances will not be taken seriously if they are expressed in plain language. Members of the new professions and branches of science are particularly vulnerable. Teaching, once a vocation, is now an elaborately structured profession in which many teachers no longer teach but administer and manage. The social sciences include as many disparate groups as the biological sciences. Today's world is one of intricate equipment, highly-developed scientific concepts and advanced or convoluted techniques in many disciplines. Rich as English is, it has not enough new words to supply these new *métiers* with terminologies of their own. New words are coined with wild abandon and terms are borrowed from other disciplines to be applied or misapplied to phenomena in new areas. Perhaps it is the rapid development of sub-sciences that makes their terminologies look like bicycles made of parts rescued from the local tip or rubbish dump. But if communication is an aspect of any such science, the use of ordinary everyday language is essential.

1.13 Comprehension should not be a matter of struggle and hard work. Information is made available through a variety of sources: textbooks, treatises, conference papers, articles in learned journals, technical specifications and advertising material. World markets and international conferences and symposia mean that much of this material will need to be translated. Translation increases opportunities for misunderstanding and misinforming. If your industry wanted to import equipment from Japan and you found that the descriptions and specifications were originally written in bad Japanese, making the translated version unintelligible, you would question the efficiency and value of the product. There is nothing sacred about the English language which makes its worst efforts acceptable in other countries.

1.14 Dictation accounts for some of the extraordinary letters sent by senior managers, government officers and heads of companies. A draft letter is gabbled into a recorder. The gist may be the message to be conveyed, but the words expressing it are just mental jottings. Secretaries are expected to type intelligible texts from the tangle; the signatories seldom seem to bother to correct or emend them. Dictated-letter addicts would often be shamed by the letters they appear to have written.

1.15 Typewriters must be blamed for some awkward writing. If a sentence starts badly or shifts out of true it is tempting to try and cobble up the mess instead of starting all over again. Writers who are neither fluent nor experienced will find it better to write the first draft by hand; it is easier to cross out mistakes.

1.16 When work is intended for publication – monographs, reports or official communications – it is often the victim of haste, carelessness or boredom. Many writers rely on the publishing house to clean up their texts. Since publishing began to suffer from rising costs and falling sales, this is no longer safe. Costs are cut by dispensing with galley proofs and putting the typescript straight into page proofs. Changes at page proof stage are expensive. Every author must take account the grim facts that alterations not due to the printer's errors have to be paid for, and that changes involving more than one line can be prohibitively costly. Unless the copy-editor, often a freelance not owing allegiance to the publisher's imprint, is vigilant and conscientious the sloppy typescript becomes the ill-written printed text.

1.17 Writers (and that term includes everyone who writes something for another to read) must obviously learn to do their homework and deal with problems themselves. One repellent factor is the language of the science. Like a man consulting a medical dictionary to determine the nature of his stomach upset, we are frightened by the terms themselves. It is worrying to discover that the discomfort one feels may be due to *dyspepsia* rather than a surfeit of sausages. Grammar, syntax and terminology sound like bogey-words, part of some abstruse branch of learning outside the boundaries of ordinary education. Often confused with each other, they are seen as invisible frontiers over which the unwary cannot help straying. Of course they are not really such barriers.

1.18 **Grammar** is the branch of learning that deals with both written and spoken language, the words used and the relationships between words. **Terminology** describes the terms used to indicate special things, events or occurrences within a particular art or science. **Syntax** is the technique of constructing sentences grammatically and is concerned with the use of words. Syntax is a practical tool and its rules, if they can be so called, deal with the application of thought and commonsense.

1.19 **Linguistics**, although a valuable science, is less useful in practical terms to the person who wants to write clearly. It is the study of the nature and development of language as a characteristic of human function and behaviour. However, it is concerned with the meanings we extract from what is said or written. The shades and small differences of meaning are especially important in the communications which take place between people separated in place and, perhaps, in time.

1.20 Avoiding an unintentional meaning can be a crucial point in written work. There will be times when it is vital not to appear insolent, offhand, patronizing, subservient or abrupt. A single word or phrase can alter the apparent message.

I am interested in the solution of the argument
tells the reader that you have a degree of personal involvement.

I am uninterested in the solution of the argument
says that you do not care what happens. But

I am disinterested in the solution of the argument
means that you are involved but in an even-handed way, not taking sides. Wherever possible I shall try to point out the 'loading' of meaning in constructions we often use.

1.21 The purpose of this book is not to lay down rigid rules but to find the points where mistakes occur most often. When you know what goes wrong and where muddles happen, you can work out how to put them right. There is no reason to suppose that laboratory rats, who are known to learn from their mistakes, are any smarter than human beings.

Not as Hard as it Looks
1.22 English derives from, and has been influenced by, highly organized languages. In these languages **nouns** were divided into groups called **declensions**, which had similar endings for use in similar and specific circumstances: possession or ownership; agency; manner; cause or reception of action. These circumstances were shown by changing the endings of the nouns, and **adjectives** attached to the nouns changed with them. These alterations are known as **inflections**, indicating particular circumstances or **cases**. **Verbs** were, in the same way, grouped into **conjugations** and had **tenses** to indicate the period of time in which action took place. **Person** showed the position and number of the noun to which the verb related. The **voice** of a verb told the hearer

or reader whether the action happened *to* someone or something or was instigated *by* them. **Mood** expressed a *wish* or *desire* that something might take place; it also delivered an *order* and expressed *conceived ideas* and *hypotheses.* .

1.23 The languages of Europe kept these inflectional systems to a greater extent. *Accidence*, the part of grammar that is concerned with inflections, has been greatly simplified in English. We have no obvious declensions and verbs are not noticeably divided into conjugations. Except for personal pronouns, gender has largely disappeared. English people do not have to contort their intellect as do the French, who must use a masculine word for a cat even when it is having kittens.

1.24 It may have been the combination of teaching languages used during successive periods in the island's history – Latin, Old English and French – that shaped English into the language known as Middle English, the forerunner of Modern English. Over time the clumsy case-endings faded away, making the language simpler. Nevertheless the simplifications required a new discipline for written English. In Latin and Germanic sentences the order of words did not matter very much as the inflections made some things obvious; the **subject, object** or **indirect object** was instantly recognizable by the ending of the word. The reader knew at once to whom or to what things happened, who or what caused the action and when it occurred. The loss of case-endings meant that another way of distinguishing between subjects and objects had to be devised.

1.25 In English the order of words has become the key. The subject is shown by its position in the sentence. **Auxiliary verbs** come in as aids to indicate more exactly the scope and time of what has occurred. Direction, position and agency are expressed by **prepositions.** The communication of thought can be managed with more variety and flexibility than in the parent languages. Although we have lost grammatical complexities, we have gained in vocabulary. English is rich in expressive terms and has, when properly used, a quality of precision.

Not as Easy as It Sounds

1.26 In Chapters Three, Four and Five the importance of case, number, person, gender, tense, mood and voice, as they still affect the language, will be discussed. Before coming to grips with the details of English grammar, however, there is an important consideration. There are two distinct areas of the language: *speech*, varying in pronunciation and construction from one region to another, and *written English*, a universal means of communication. Dialect, which is colourful and interesting to hear, nevertheless represents the speech pattern of only one part of the country and may be unintelligible outside it. Speakers throughout the country, from North to South, schoolchildren, assembly-line workers, politicians and broadcasters, fling words together with unconcerned abandon, secure in the knowledge that they will be understood by their immediate neighbours. In a face-to-face situation some of the problems posed by regional speech and idioms can be overcome by using gestures, frowns and smiles.

1.27 But to believe that merely to speak English is a qualification for writing is to be as self-deluded as the black cat that thinks it is invisible when it shuts its eyes. Nor can classes in Creative English produce fluency and clarity when they are intended as exercises in self-expression. Without case, person and tense written English would become a form of Pidgin and be just as cumbersome. Written English is a subject on its own, involving a command of words (vocabulary), an understanding of word usage and relationships (grammar) and an ability to construct sentences (syntax). Even when you are writing a memo or answering an examination question, you are an interpreter, translating thoughts into words with the purpose of making yourself understood.

Chapter Two
Making a start

2.1 Literate adults are expected to be able to manage more complicated prose than is needed for notes to the milkman. The pursuit of knowledge for the sheer pleasure of learning is satisfying but does not provide an income. Most of us are educated for some occupation and every occupation carries with it its own measure of written communication. It may be no more than letters to people who have not paid their bills; on the other hand you may wish to write a publishable thesis or be asked to describe equipment you have designed.

2.2 Once the written message has left your hands, it must speak for itself. If you have botched the job of writing, it is too late to alter the consequences. Even the milkman's note needs to carry a clear unequivocal meaning. If you just put 'More milk', you could have a front garden full of the stuff. Like any operation requiring precision, you need tools for the job and a system of working.

Books – Tools for the Job
2.3 Everyone comes unstuck at some time. Even people who study linguistics can make mistakes. The difference between the grammarian and the ordinary educated writer is that the professional finds it easier to recognize mistakes, ambiguities and false constructions. The skilled mechanic will still refer to the handbook for the car on which he is working. He will use a reference book and so should the educated writer.

2.4 Reference books are essential items for everyone who wants to communicate in writing. They are the *batterie de cuisine* or tools for the job. Just as you would not take a washing machine apart without the manual that shows how it can be put together again, it is sensible to have some sort of help at hand when you start to put words on paper. The most important tool is a dictionary. Any old dictionary will not do. You need one that will do more than help your spelling and define words. In Appendix I you will find the title of one that will show the grammatical constructions into which many words fit, giving particular associations with prepositions and showing which verbs do or do not take objects. As it needs to be always at hand, it must be your own property. Buy it.

2.5 When you wish to borrow or buy a book, you should be able to give the librarian or bookseller the full details. Appendix I lists books that ought to be on everybody's bookshelf, as well as those which are useful enough to own and those that you may wish to borrow.

2.6 Appendix I also has a list of more specialized books, academic works on grammar and syntax, books dealing with linguistics and some concerned with particular areas of grammar. These are for people seriously intending to study structure and usage. The writer who wishes merely to avoid mistakes could be sucked down into the shifting sands of individual terminology and the symbols and codifications of linguistics and need not confuse herself or himself with them.

Traps and quicksands
2.7 There are some books you should avoid at all costs until you have developed a capacity for writing clear English. These are books written for foreign visitors and students and their purpose is to explain contemporary malapropisms, mispronunciations and mangled grammar in English **colloquial speech.** They may be a boon to tourists but used by the English as handbooks they reinforce and perpetuate mistakes, and are worse than useless.

2.8 Similarly, dictionaries of slang, or those marked 'modern' or giving American usage, are not, for the writer beginning to master his or her craft, helpful as general reference books. Have them by all means, but your first dictionary should be the one listed in Appendix I.

2.9   At this point I begin to hear the thundering hooves of those who believe that, to preserve our heritage of dialect, there should be no standardization of the way in which English is written. Before I am trampled flat, I must say once more that dialect is a valuable part of the study of *spoken* English. It has nothing to do with *written* English, except as dialogue in works of fiction. Written English is a totally separate subject and, if it is to be understood by any reader, must have some standardization of usage and construction.

The Skeleton of Work — the Outline

2.10   Nothing annoys a reader more than a piece of writing in which the ideas are confused and presented out of order. Bear in mind that everything that is written, no matter how trivial, represents a human agent; words are put on paper by people. Even if the words are jumbled and mis-spelt, they stand for something you wished to say and what you have written may be a permanent record. Try never to let anything leave your hands that might later shame you.

2.11   Before you begin to write, organize your ideas and decide what must be said about the subject. This decision includes what you need *not* say about the subject; too much information can be as offputting as being served the water with the cabbage. Strain off everything that is irrelevant and remember to include anything that is necessary.

2.12   Defining the limits of the subject serves two purposes: it enables you to concentrate on the area you wish to cover and it helps you to avoid being side-tracked. You should also remind yourself of the person or persons you are addressing, be it an examiner, a pupil, a client or the managing director.

2.13   The first step is to make an outline. This does not commit you to anything – it is only a useful guide and a reminder. Make two or three if you want to — each time you will come closer to establishing the right shape for your work. Your aim must be to avoid muddle, the sort of jumbled text that makes the reader waste time picking brussels sprouts out of the custard and rescuing the apple pie from the gravy.

2.14 The purpose of an outline is to make the writer think about the communication of ideas effectively rather than just showing off knowledge. If you were asked to describe a spiral staircase to someone who had never seen a second-storied house, could you do so? Without using your hands? Without using the words 'helix' or 'circular'? Would you remember to say *why* one would use a spiral stair instead of a conventional form? Try describing something more difficult: a helicopter and its movement. Do not let yourself use the word 'rotor' without explaining the nature of a rotor. In the same way, you will have to define 'thrust', 'lift', 'drag' and 'angle of attack', and have a clear idea of the order in which these concepts should be introduced.

2.15 It is a good exercise to describe familiar objects in this way; it makes one aware of the difference between exposition and mere communication. To plunge straight in, flapping hands and saying 'what I mean' and 'you know' exposes one's deficiencies; one may not be as smart as one thinks. Success depends on stopping to think before you begin to speak. Most of us need practice in doing so. When you have something to be written down, it is even more important to collect your wits and arrange facts.

2.16 A habit of thinking and working in outline form can be useful in terms of time and length. Where essential points must be put over in the right sequence in a limited time, the outline can be used without any additions. If, on the other hand, the examination answer, essay or report must be of a required length the initial outline is a framework on which to build.

Headings
2.17 An outline is divided into sections under *headings*. Headings should play a vital part in the assembly of your argument. As you set down each one, think about its relevance to the one before it and the one that follows. You are

looking for the order that best fits your subject. A good case or clear exposition can be spoilt if you have not worked out the best logical sequence for presenting the points you must cover.

2.18 Sometimes fresh material has to be incorporated. New information becomes available while you are writing, or you realize that there are ideas bordering on your main theme which are relevant enough to be inserted. The headings in your outline should show you where these ideas can be inserted without disturbing the path of your subject.

2.19 The main parts or broad areas of the subject are put down first under *main headings*. Suppose you must give a picture of slugs for someone who knows little about them apart from their appetite and slime.

Title: SLUGS
    I. The animal family to which slugs belong;
   II. Where slugs live;
  III. What slugs are like;
  IV. The food slugs eat;
   V. How slugs move;
  VI. How slugs breed.

Sub-headings
2.20 Details are covered by sub-headings. In a formal outline all headings are given a code or letter. There is a generally accepted order in which they are used: Roman numerals, capital letters, Arabic numerals and lower case letters. The order is known as *weighting*. In preparing an outline it is useful if you are able to refer to, say, III C 2 a and know that you or anyone reading the outline can find the reference easily. Here is a main heading with sub-headings under it:

  III. What slugs are like:
    A. Size;
    B. Head:
      1. mouth
        a. tongue and teeth;

      2. 'feelers';
      3. eyes;
  C. Body:
      1. back;
      2. mantle;
        a. mantle 'pore';
      3. foot;
  D. Skin;
  E. Glands.

The reference III C 2 a takes you to the mantle 'pore'.

2.21 You may, of course, be writing for readers already familiar with the animal: a paper or article, an examination answer or essay. For an example of this sort, take the title LOCOMOTION IN SLUGS. Use technical terms where they avoid longwindedness.

   I. Types of movement;
  II. Muscularity:
    A. dorso-ventral
    B. transverse and longitudinal;
 III. Glands:
    A. foot epithelium
    B. pedal;
 IV. Mechanism of locomotion:
    A. hydraulic
    B. adhesive.

2.22 As you add the sub-headings, examine your work for balance. Make sure that the important items of information or argument are evenly distributed and lead into one another naturally. It can be tempting to mass the strongest points and present them in a heap as soon as possible, in case the reader may be too impatient to read on. Your argument or theme should, instead, grow in strength or build up point by point until it reaches the clinching statement, summary or conclusion.

2.23 For people writing work that is to be published, making an outline serves yet another purpose. You may want to use headings above paragraphs or sections in the finished work to show their importance or to introduce a new topic or sub-topic. All too often writers just put in headings without giving their hierarchical significance. It is then the unfortunate copy-editor who has to decide how they shall be set, showing the weighting by placing the code for the printer next to each one. Authors sometimes complain that headings were set with more or less emphasis than was needed to show their importance. The fault is theirs. The conscientious author, especially one who started with an outline, indicates the weight of each heading and does not expect someone to make his or her decisions.

Beginning

2.24 Where do you begin? At the beginning, of course, but things are seldom as simple as they sound. Even the most experienced writers find it difficult to get into a subject from a standing start. One solution is to begin by writing down *something*, even if it has little to do with the subject. Try putting the date at the top of the paper and then get your-self moving by rambling a little, writing whatever comes into your head. Struggle on until you have warmed up as you are bound to do if you really know your subject. When the work is complete and you are revising, discard the original 'warm-up' sentences. You will probably find an appropriate sen-tence later in the first paragraphs. If not you are still in a better position to compose a more attractive beginning.

2.25 A number of factors have to be taken into account. If the subject is to be covered in a large and general way, the reader may need background material, perhaps the history of previous actions or an introduction to the nature of the subject. Often the precise starting point is determined for you, as in the third example: LOCOMOTION IN SLUGS. If your theme is a specific part of a larger subject and your readers will be well-informed, you can plunge straight in, though it is still worth taking trouble to find an interesting introduction. At times, a quotation can provide a starting point; after all, the vicar begins his sermon with a text.

2.26 It is a sensible precaution to remember that the

reader is a human being with human interests and reactions.* Communication between readers and writers is like a game for two players in which the writer has the more active, and probably more interesting, part. Think of the reader as a diffident or unwilling partner who needs to be coaxed to play. There can be no hanging about; the reader will slope off if you waste time. His or her involvement is directly related to your desire to play the game. Unless you have an interest in or, even better, an enthusiasm for the subject the game will never begin. You must grab attention. You must also let the reader see the subject, declaring the name of the game to which he or she is being enticed.

2.27　In the 1930s the University of Chicago produced textbooks that were fascinating reading for any layman but were also serious scientific manuals. A student lucky enough to have Ralph Buchsbaum's textbook on invertebrates, *Animals without Backbones*, was told in the first sentence that anyone could tell the difference between a tree and a cow. That statement was expanded in the first paragraph to give the reader the basis of the difference: the way in which they fed. By the third paragraph the serious subject of the book, invertebrate animals, was firmly established.

2.28　To sum up, always regard your space as limited and the reader's time as precious. Try to make the opening sentence interesting but absolutely relevant to your subject. Here are two invitations to read on:

> One does not normally regard a kitchen as having much in common with a laboratory.
>
> > Steven Rose: *The Chemistry of Life*,
> > Penguin Books (1966)

and

> An epidendron is a plant that cannot stand up for itself, relying on a tree for support and shelter, but is, like a good colonist, otherwise self-sufficient.

---

* The National Geographic Society and other institutions have supported research into communication with gorillas and chimpanzees, but readership among those animals is inconsiderable. For the next 30 years or so, you will do better addressing someone fashioned like yourself.

2.29 The words with which you begin tell the readers something about you. The first sentence can show whether you know your subject and are confident in your ability to write about it. It also displays your judgement (or lack of it) about the readers you are addressing. You may appear to be facetious, boring or merely uncertain. Avoid beginnings like

> It is generally agreed;
> From time to time;
> It occurs to me;
> For those who are interested;

Waffling starts like these indicate that you are afraid readers will not take you seriously. They almost certainly mean that there will be little inclination to read on. The last example, for instance, inevitably induces the reaction 'not me, for one'. The writer has to get right in, head, hand and pen.

Flesh on the Bones

2.30 Communicating by writing is hard work. There are few people to whom it comes naturally but many find that it is worth the effort to master it. Dr Johnson, who spent most of his life at it, said: 'What is written without effort is in general read without pleasure.'

2.31 When the boundaries of the subject have been set and the outline prepared, the work of filling and covering begins. If you just pour out an uncontrolled flood of words you will bury your subject, bones and all. Some control of composition is necessary and, if you wish never to have to apologize for the way you write, some quality as well. The hallmark of quality is simplicity. The simplest way of reaching out to the reader is the best.

Sentences

2.32 It is sensible to prefer short sentences to express yourself simply. But written work can be boring if it is made up entirely of short sentences. It can affect the pace of reading as a flight of shallow steps affects walking: the rhythm is uncomfortable. The mode of expression is the language you speak. Write as naturally for the reader as if you were talking about the subject and the reader will absorb what you say as naturally. Vary the length of sentences as you would in speech. Long sentences need not be involved or difficult. There is nothing about written thought that requires it to be pompous or stilted.

2.33   You are looking for a rhythm that is appealing and avoids boredom. To test the rhythm of your work, read it aloud. If it is jerky and uncomfortable to read, if it does not flow as easily as speech, you need to rewrite it. At the same time, you must take care not to incorporate any bad habits you use when talking – unfinished sentences that tail away into a wave of the hand, or a peppering of written 'ers' and 'ums' like 'you know', 'I mean to say' and 'well'.

Paragraphs
2.34   Sentences are complete statements. Paragraphs are groups of complete statements that fit together around a single line of thought. Sentences are grouped in paragraphs to help the reader see your path through your subject matter and to make sure that he or she is not faced with an unbroken stream of sentences. Pages filled from top to bottom and side to side with words can put off even the most dedicated reader.

2.35   Wherever possible keep paragraphs short. But the *length* of a paragraph is not the reason for its existence; appearance matters less than content. A paragraph is a collection of related sentences, forming a revetment for part of your theme or a point in your argument. If the next sentence you are about to write carries the thought of the last one on, it belongs in the same paragraph. If it starts a new chain of ideas it should be the beginning of a new paragraph.

2.36   Try not to let length get out of hand. Swollen paragraphs and a great many sentences about one small part of your topic may show that you have overdone it. Are all the sentences really necessary?

Choosing your words

2.37   Use the right word for the job. The simple word is usually the best. Using a long involved word when there is a shorter equivalent merely sounds pompous. This doesn't mean that you are confined to monosyllables; complex words do have their place. There are times when a long word or a technical term must be used because it is the only one that expresses your meaning. What you avoid are the pen-pusher's props, the badge of 'officialese':

(a) simple terms rather than 'genteelisms':

use	**not**	utilize
begin		commence
or	**not**	or
start		originate
before	**not**	prior to
many	**not**	numerous
needs	**not**	requirements

(b) positive words rather than sidesteps:

go	**not**	proceed
stop	**not**	deter
scarce	**not**	in short supply

2.38   The strength of a statement can be weakened by trimming it up. It gains little or nothing from the number of words used:

Weak:	*Strong:*
According to whether	} If
In the event of	
At the present time	Now
In order to	To
In spite of the fact that	} Although
Allowing for	
Give assurances that	Promise

In view of ⎫	Since
As a result ⎭	
In regard to ⎫	About
In connection with ⎭	
For the reason that ⎫	Because
Owing to the fact that ⎭	
Make/have an impact on	Impress
In the first instance	First
A certain amount of	Some
From time to time ⎫	Sometimes
As circumstances arise ⎭	
During such time	While
In order that	So that
It is clear that	Clearly
It is obvious that	Obviously
On the basis of	Based on
Meet up with	Meet
Take into consideration	Consider
Make an attempt	Try

Never forget that you expose yourself to the reader when you write. The weak phrases give the impression of uncertainty. They have an apologetic look.

Fancy dress

2.39 Some words and phrases are chosen because the writer believes that they make his work more convincing and give it an academic air. Too often they make it seem as if he is showing off, and being pretentious. A pig with feathers behind its ears is still a pig and not a bird of paradise. Steer clear of heavy-handed clichés and 'puffed-up' words:

> With reference to
> The ultimate objective
> The attending circumstances
> The prevailing conditions
> A substantial proportion
> The inescapable conclusion

Writing 'an extensive bibliography' may make you proud to

have spelt it correctly, but a 'long booklist' means the same thing. Do not say 'aggregate' if what you really mean is 'sum'. Avoid 'appreciating' if you can 'understand'; and never have a 'concept' where you could have had an 'idea'. If you are short of money or equipment, say so; try not to be mealy-mouthed about 'limited resources'. Whatever the temptation, never allow yourself to say 'at this moment in time'. Everyone will know that you watch too many politicians on television.

Technical terms

2.40   Every true science has its technical terms. They are used to express complex ideas, systems or actions and they are both useful and necessary. But when you are writing you should use them only where

(a) there is no simple alternative;
(b) the reader is sure to understand them.

The two sentences below followed each other in a textbook for biochemistry students. The first explained the idea of the 'steady state' in simple terms. The second applied that idea to the discipline in which the textbook was to be used.

1. The population of a country is in a steady state when the birth and immigration rates equal those of death and emigration.
2. The concentration of a metabolite in the cell is at a steady-state level when it is being produced as rapidly as it is being degraded.

> Fersht: *Enzyme Structure and Metabolism*,
> Freeman, 1977

2.41   Now look at the next two examples, taken from different parts of a set of specifications. The writer is trying to make his descriptions definite and unambiguous. One wonders what his non-technical readers made of it.

1. All data may be designated as preferred by the input processing function when requested by manual input from the supervisory position.

2. The transmission of (these) messages shall be supported by a communications protocol which includes the provision for acceptance and rejection messages and re-transmission attempts when failures occur.

The first sentence was meant to tell the customer that the supervisor can push a button to alter and control information. The second informed him that message transmission had a system that included ways of accepting, rejecting and sending messages again.

Pace

2.42   You can regulate the pace and vitality of work by the sort of words you use. Direct and active statements have more life than indirect statements. Using transitive verbs (**4.45–6**) and the active voice (**4.47–8**) will have a positive, enlivening, effect when you want to convey something vividly.

> Dalglish, a master of work, created all three goals. In the seventeenth minute he released Nicol ... and steered the loose ball for his thirteenth goal of the relatively young season before Everton's defence could think about recovery. ... By now Everton ... were so comprehensively outplayed that to touch the ball was a welcome surprise.
>
> *The Times*

Notice how the pace changes from the rapid succession of *created, released* and *steered*, all verbs in the active voice, taking objects, to the more sober *were so outplayed*, where the passive voice gives a sense of finality.

Meaning

2.43   Never use a word if you do not know exactly what it means. In a later chapter words often misused or misunderstood will be discussed. The following words should send you to the dictionary (look them up now!):

a priori/posteriori	factitious	premiss(es)
aggravate	feasible	progressive
alternate	fictitious	proven
alternative	fortuitous	radical
ambience	imply	refute
anticipate	infer	renege
appreciate	media	scenario
comprise	militate	sensual
crisis	mitigate	sensuous
crucial	modest	transpire
decimate	paranoia	viable
disinterested	paranoid	*vis-à-vis*

Presentation

2.44 If you keep your clothes in a heap under the bed, it may prove difficult to arrive at a party looking suave and elegant. The way in which you treat your work as it progresses can have an effect on the finished product.

2.45 If ideas come sporadically, file them under the appropriate heading. The simplest way to do this is to use a loose-leaf binder filled with plastic pockets which you can get at any stationery shop. Stick a label on each pocket to indicate the section to which the notes apply and put all jottings into the pocket. When you flesh out the outline from your notes, draw a line across each one to show that it has been used and put it in a box – a shoebox will do, though you may need a larger one for manuscript pages after the material has been typed.

2.46 If the work is to be printed, the publisher will supply a copy of the house style notes, showing how books under the imprint are to be set out. If you are responsible for printing, see your typesetter before the manuscript is typed and agree on a style. In that case, you will need to discuss the typeface to be used, the size of type and the way in which headings are to be set. Try not to use more than three weights of headings. Academic authors tend to indulge in minute distinctions and lots of sub-headings. These only confuse the reader and make difficulties for the typesetter. They also increase the time taken to set and put up the cost.

2.47   If a chapter falls naturally into two or three parts, too closely related to form separate chapters, they can be designated as 'Chapter 0 – Part I' and 'Chapter 0 – Part II'. If the chapter head is in large or bold type, then the parts can be set in small, even capitals. The usual headings are *main*, shown as A in the margin, and two weights of sub-heading, shown as B and C. Look at the headings in this book to see one way of distinguishing weights.

2.48   The typescript must have a generous left-hand margin and be at least double-spaced on A4 paper. If your typewriter has a 1–2–3–4–5 setting for spacing, use 3. You need to space so that a correction line can be typed in between the lines without impinging on them. Try to make sure that margins and tabulation are the same throughout the typescript.

2.49   Be consistent. The writer who chops and changes the system of headings and alters terminology and spelling, or gives the same reference in a dozen different ways, may be a lovable eccentric to his or her friends but is merely a thundering nuisance to the editor and typesetter. Choose the way in which you use headings, terms, titles or references and stick to it.

2.50   If you are employing a typist, please make sure that he or she reads the style notes and sets the pages out in the right way. It is both arrogant and ignorant to expect someone else to clean up your messy manuscript or typescript and correct your mistakes. Often it is the writer who sends in the most dog-eared, scribbled-over typescript, typed with single spacing and no margins, who expects the printed book to be an accurate representation of what was in his or her mind.

2.51   Never have less than two copies of the typescript. You should really have three copies or, in some instances, four. All copies must be marked and corrected in exactly the same way. Don't make notes on one copy without marking the others. Then the folios or pages in each copy must be numbered identically. This is very important and the typescript must not be sent off before you have done this. It is the only way in which telephone discussions with the editor or typesetter can be related to the proper section of your work.

2.52 If the work you are engaged on requires more research than was expected, if you fall ill – or if you are cut off for weeks by an avalanche – you may not be able to meet your deadline. The editor may have allowed contingency time or made more than enough provision for extensive editing. Nevertheless you *must* let the editor know as soon as you realise that you will not be ready by the date agreed between you. It is still your duty to make every effort and be single-minded to try and finish on time.

The genie of the microchip

2.53 Many of us are bewitched by the idea of a robot that would write for us; like cats looking wistfully at washing machines – how convenient it would be to have one's fur mechanically laundered instead of licking it laboriously with one's tongue – we think of avoiding hard labour. A word-processor sounds like the awkward writer's dream, a device for turning muddled thoughts into pellucid prose and sparkling sentences. Unfortunately the oddly-named word-processor will do nothing of the sort. It is an aid to efficiency; combining the functions of a self-correcting electric typewriter and an electronic printer, it provides a better method of revising, editing and correcting and it will produce many extra copies of the finished work. What it will not do is to compose written work for you.

2.54 The efficacy of a word-processor depends on efficient use. Because it can be used to recall and rearrange any part of the text, it requires a greater mental compass and a thorough knowledge of the mechanics of writing. If you row in a dinghy, you must pull at the oars yourself; in a galley, you exchange the work of rowing for the work of managing and controlling a group of galley slaves. Employ a word-processor as the excellent editing tool that it is when you know what you are doing. Don't expect it to eliminate effort or to make up for basic ignorance.

Chapter Three
Facts, ideas and images

3.1   Clear communication relies on more than neatness and good presentation. Words are the medium of expressing thought. English speakers cannot trust to their ears alone but must have an understanding of the words they use. Like the man who wrote to an adversary

> I insist on having a site of the brief you sent to your solicitor

you may be unintentionally guilty of ignorance when you only meant to be guilty of rudeness. Joining words together by ear without being sure of their meaning, or the part they play in sentences, can make nonsense.

3.2   The dishevelled statement needs a lot of interpretation.

> Another major area of bolt-on goodies are connected with carburation and exhaust.

What sort of word is *area* – does it mean more than one thing? How is *connected* used – is something physically joined to something else? Do *bolt-on goodies* fall into a particular group or category? What about *carburation* and *exhaust*? One describes a process and the other seems not to make sense in the context. Would we understand the statement better if it were reworded?

> Carburettors and exhaust systems are the major kinds of bolt-on goodies.

3.3   On the other hand, writers who recognize the use of words are easily understood.

> The worms live inside the tubes, with their heads at the bottom of the burrow feeding on the mud while their tails wave about in the water.
>
> Mellanby: Animal Life in Fresh Water,
Methuen (1938)

3.4   Words that have different functions in sentences are divided into classes, known collectively as the parts of speech, the subject of this chapter and the next. They are like groups of jigsaw puzzle shapes, subdivided by the part of the picture that appears on their surfaces. Words, however, can be put together to form an infinite number of pictures though, like puzzle pieces, they can be jammed or damaged by clumsy or impetuous hands. All you are left with then is a collection of rubbish.

3.5   When we write about something, that something is our subject. A fly, which can be seen, heard and squashed, is a matter-of-fact subject; Cartesianism, a philosophical system, is an abstract subject or idea; both are nouns. The subject of every sentence is a noun and to make its meaning or image clearer we add articles, adjectives and adverbs.

Nouns
3.6   Nouns are the building blocks of language. They are the code words we use to identify everything about us. Since language, written or spoken, is the basic medium of communication it must begin by naming what we know: people, places, animals, inanimate objects, intangibles, emotions and states of mind. Slang words and jargon show the need to name things even when the speaker or writer may be unaware of, or indifferent to, words that are already there. Without nouns we should have to point to things and grunt. Writing would be impossible.

The two Oxford dictionaries, Shorter and Concise, define a noun as 'a word used as the name of a person or thing'. Some grammarians prefer the word **substantive**, a rather ponderous term to cover words like *courage, laughter* and *air*, although it seems appropriate for *lead* and *elephant*. Let nouns be nouns for most of our purposes.

Noun classes
3.7   Nouns are classified in four groups:
Proper nouns that identify individual people or particular
    places and objects: Dr Hills, Kermit, Paris, the Rosetta

Stone. Proper nouns always begin with a capital letter;

Common nouns indicate something in a wide range of objects without identifying one in particular: teapot, teacher, telephone, tree;

Abstract nouns cover feelings, states, virtues, intangibles – all that we cannot see: terror, poverty, infinity, faith.

Collective nouns identify groups of people, animals or things: group, flock, gaggle, crowd, heap, regiment. These nouns are also called *nouns of multitude* and include some that can be treated as singular or plural, though never both ways in the same sentence. You can write 'The Council does not know its own mind'; or this can be 'The Council do not know their own minds' but *not* 'The Council does not know their own minds'. Collective nouns behave irregularly and this is shown in paragraph **3.8** (8–9).

Number

3.8   English nouns have lost most of the inflections inherited from the parent languages, but we have kept the change relating to number. When a noun refers to more than one of a kind, it usually changes from the singular form to the plural. Most forms are familiar to us from daily use throughout our lives:

1. Plural forms with an added *s*: goat – goats;
2. Those which add *es*: mattress – mattresses;
3. Those that change the ending: thief – thieves; calf – calves;
4. Those that change the vowel after the first letter: louse – lice; man – men; goose – geese;
5. Reminders of Old English: children; brethren; oxen;
6. Some that have the same form in the singular and the plural: sheep; deer; counsel; trout; salmon;
7. Some words have special applications. They have an *s* plural but are used in the singular form when teamed with a number. Some take a plural verb; others are singular: fifteen stone *is* a heavy weight; there *are* five couple of hounds in the pack; one dozen *is* quite enough; there *are* thirty head of cattle in the ring. Although some words normally have a plural form they

can act as a collective when used without *s*: a cran of fish; shooting duck.

8. Most of the collective nouns in **3.8**(7) have ordinary plurals: Council – Councils; government – governments; army – armies.

9. Plural irregularities:

(a) Some words with *s* or *es* are immutably plural: thanks *are* due; riches *were* amassed; alms *are* given; the tongs *are* missing;

(b) Others are always plural without an *s*: clergy; cattle; police; brace; gross; kindred;

(c) One group, with *s*, is usually plural, but can be used in the singular: bellows; means; by *this* means – using *these* means; to set up *a* headquarters – the headquarters *are* near;

(d) Some are primarily singular but can be used as plural: a gallows *was* put up on the village green; gallows *were* put up on many village greens; the room is *a* shambles; shambles *were* the forerunners of modern abattoirs.

10. Singularities: Writers are often undecided about the number of certain singular nouns. Those which end in *s* present obvious problems, but one can use the *substitution* principle; when in doubt, try another word in the sentence:

(a) How should one treat 'measles' or 'mathematics'? Try

Diphtheria is a very serious disease

and you can see that we must write

Measles *is* a very serious disease,

never

Measles are controlled by vaccination.

A common mistake is

Mathematics are essential subjects.

No one would write

Geography are essential subjects.

The confusion is deepened by references to 'the branches of mathematics', increasing our feeling that it ought to be a collective noun. And so, in certain cases, it can be: *the higher mathematics*, as you see, require a plural verb. When it is a subject, however, like 'needlework'

Mathematics *is* an essential subject.

Watch the verb form you use with 'physics', another subject that ends in *s*. 'Gymnastics' and 'callisthenics' are singular when the *subject* appears in the curriculum but can be plural when you refer to the exercises.

(b) There are other collective nouns which are always singular, among them: machinery; soldiery;

(c) And certain abstract nouns have no plural. Examples are: laughter; courage; haste; wisdom; behaviour.

Although *behaviour* has the definitive meaning of 'conduct' and 'the actions, activities, manners and bearing relating to a person's general conduct', psychologists have adopted *behaviour* as professional jargon for individual aspects of behaviour. This has led them to invent a gross plural, *behaviours*, to cover the precise meaning of the original singular word. This sort of junk word is harmless when used among two or three psychologists gathered together or among members of a professional coven. The damage is done when social workers, teachers and lay persons seize on the misuse and adopt it as a badge of knowledge.

How shall we replace *behaviour* as a specific term for the sum of actions, conduct and deportment if it is to be ignorantly used to mean any one of those actions, any aspect of that conduct or deportment and then turned into a new plural form to regain its original meaning? The loss of, or damage to, a word through carelessness impoverishes the language.

11. Perpetual puzzles: what is the plural of 'spoonful'? That depends on how many spoons you have. Take one spoon and fill it; you have one spoonful. Add it to the cake or swallow the dose and fill it again. Repeat the action and you have added two *spoonfuls* to the mixture

or taken the prescribed dose. A *spoonful* is a measure. Filling two or more spoons, you could write of *spoons full*, but that would describe their number and contents, not the quantity they held. Adding 'ful' to 'hand' we have formed a new noun that has its own plural:

> handful – handfuls; spoonful – spoonfuls.

12. *Number* and *majority* pose special problems. If a roof has a quantity of loose slates, may one say

> A number of slates *are* loose?

Yes. And in

> The raised hands made it clear that the majority *were* in favour,

the plural verb is correct. In the first example, there is a compound subject, *number of slates*, and in the second, *majority* is used to represent the greater number of *persons* voting. On the other hand, if you want to describe the *number*, rather than the *slates*, number is singular.

> The number of loose slates is large.

If you use *majority* in the abstract sense, to describe the decision rather than the people making the decision, it is a singular **noun of multitude.**

> The majority *was* sufficient to pass the resolution.

The distinction is between the number or quantity (abstract) and the number of tangible things (concrete) when you are deciding whether to use a singular or plural verb. *Majority* is treated in the same way, but also has a 'middle' sense, as a noun of multitude when, like *crowd* it can be singular or plural:

> The crowd was angry:
> The crowd were angry,

as long as you remain consistent, continuing to treat it as singular or plural in the same context; you are treating it as a single many-headed creature *or* a number of individuals. Choose one and stick to it.

Gender

3.9 English people find the gender of European nouns difficult to master. Since our ancestors abandoned gender in nouns long ago it no longer seems natural. French words are masculine or feminine because of their classical origins and not, as one might suppose, because of a perverse desire to torment foreigners. As the gender is unrelated to the meaning of the word, it only becomes apparent when the article and any adjectives attached to the noun are in a masculine or feminine form: *La belle table est mise.* It leads to some absurdities, like the French female billy-goat, from which we are preserved.

3.10 **Gender** and **meaning** should not be thought of as hand in hand. Although many English nouns identify people and animals as male or female, the identification lies in the definition of the word; the noun is without gender. The only agreement to be found in an English sentence occurs when the noun is an antecedent for a pronoun. A noun that defines the gender of the person referred to, for example, 'actress', will need the feminine pronouns *she* and *her*.

3.11 It is worth making a distinction, however, between the words that have gender as an intrinsic meaning and those that fall into the dog-walking-on-its-hind-legs category. *Goddess, abbess* and *duchess* give us information about the sex of the person that is relevant to the position, vocation or office held; but *editress, authoress, poetess* and *patroness* suggest that these are people whose work or standing is judged by their performance as women, not on the merit of what they do. An *actress* needs to have it known that she can play Electra but would essay Hamlet only as a curiosity. Being female is important to her professionally. On the other hand it is patronizing to call a writer an *authoress* or *poetess* when her sex has nothing to do with the standard by which such work is measured.

Case in nouns

3.12 Each word in a sentence stands in a particular relationship to the other words. In the classical languages, Ancient

Greek and Latin, the circumstances affecting nouns and pronouns were shown by **case endings**. We differentiated the word *table* in

(1) The table is large

from

(2) I brought food to the table

and

(3) He hit me with the table.

by changing the shape of the word (**inflecting** it) to show that in (1) *table* was the subject of the sentence; in (2) it was the indirect object; and in (3) it was the thing *by* or *with which* the action was performed. The simplification of English over the centuries swept most of these changes or endings away. Nouns have (apart from constructions relating to circumstances, which we will look at later) only one distinct case left. In every other instance, as you can see from the examples, the form of the word is the same, whatever the context. The one remaining case in nouns is the **genitive**, or **possessive** case.

Noun possessives

3.13   It is always possible to express possession by saying

the paw of the monkey; the pyjamas of the cat.

Constructions of that sort have their uses but are too stilted and unwieldy for use in every instance. So the noun is **inflected** by adding *s* after an apostrophe:

the monkey's paw; the cat's pyjamas.

So far, so good. But some come to grief when confronted by words with their own *s* ending that are in the genitive case. Donkeys, for example, are awkward and unmanageable beasts, even on paper. Start with a possessive singular:

the ass's ears; the bee's knees.

The ordinary plural would be

asses; bees

but if we add another *s* we can feel a disagreeable buzzing:

the asses's ears; the bees's knees.

Be comforted; it is no more necessary to write the words with those extra *s* sounds than it is to say them as 'beezes' or 'assezes'. We put in the apostrophe and leave out the *s*:

the asses' ears; the bees' knees; the snakes' skins.

There is an exception to this practice. Proper nouns are allowed the full dignity of that extra *s*, however it may sound:

St James's; Silas's; Charles's; Miss Adams's.

But we never say or write *Jesus's*. That possessive is *of Jesus* or simply *Jesus'*.

3.14 *Progress or regression?* In a language that is always committed to the process of change, can we find a good reason for the use of the apostrophe and *s*? If one alternative is considered, for example *the Mary-book* instead of *Mary's book*, the simplification is obvious but the gain in comprehension is doubtful. The alternative is no shorter and the unadorned *Mary-* looks like an adjective.

Languages, like communities, grow organically, with changes that are slow but always related to understanding. No matter how attractive introduced changes may seem, they fail if the alteration is understood by only a small percentage of the language-users.

The argument for keeping the apostrophe and *s* lies in their history. It is not an arbitrary use of punctuation; the apostrophe marks an abbreviation. Ben Jonson, in his *Grammar* of 1692, refers to the 'gross syntax of the *Pronoun his* joining with a Noun', a form that persisted until the beginning of the last century, though its use had diminished considerably with the passage of time. It can still be found as an archaism today on some book-plates:

Ben Jonson his book.

While Jonson's first *Grammar* (1640) did not show the abbreviation, by 1692 he could commend the new usage, which had won general acceptance. It is the simplest solution and it would be hard to find a better one.

Articles

3.15 *Little words of some account.* You may well wonder what anyone could find to say about articles, those inconsiderable words. *The, a* and *an* have been so much part of our expressive vocabulary since we began to talk that we use them automatically. Yet they are words that can round out the meaning of a sentence when used with deliberation. The function of the definite and indefinite articles is to enable the reader to distinguish between one of a general group or collection of objects and one object in particular.

A soap factory manufactures soap;
The soap factory produced black smoke.

They also serve, by their omission, to expand the scope of the subject:

Soap factories can be unpleasant workplaces;
Man cannot live by bread alone.

The flexibility is possible because the English definite article, *the*, is used in a positive, restrictive, way. This flexibility is denied to the French, for instance. Compare

pomp and circumstance

with

l'éclat et la circonstance.

The second sentence is not a French idiom but a literal translation. Notice how the English version encompasses *all* pomp and *all* circumstance, giving an abstract image of splendour and display. The French sentence is much weaker because the articles must be included to show the gender of the nouns.

In this sentence:

Elizabeth II has been Queen since 1952

attention is focused on the Queen as a person. But if it were written as:

> Elizabeth II has been the Queen since 1952

the emphasis is transferred to the monarchy with Her Majesty as incumbent or reigning monarch; the meaning is concerned with the State, not the person. If we read of

> the Bronte sisters

it is plain that we should recognize them as well-known characters.

3.16 Articles, then, are useful pointers. *Time*, obviously, represents an abstract concept; *the time* is the immediate present, shown by *a timepiece; a time to mourn* is a specified period but not related to a particular date or hour. These distinctions convey information without writing it all out.

3.17 On the other hand, the indefinite articles *a* and *an* are used with less restriction in English than in German or French. In European languages they imply emphasis, while we pepper our conversation with them:

> I think I'll have an orange;
> Did you have a good day?
> It came apart with a bang;
> They gave a party for me;
> A dog ran across the grass.

I plan to eat just one orange; the day is one known to both speaker and hearer; the bang is related to the dissolution of the object, and so on.

3.18 We could use either article in the following sentence and it would be quite sensible:

> (1) On a fine May evening, friends met;
> (2) On the fine May evening, the friends met.

We have a subtle shift of meaning from (1), which is intro-ductory and establishes a time of day and of year with an added sense of chance encounter, to (2) which indicates one particular evening and implies a prearranged meeting. In the same way,

> the man on the horse

may be the one who kicked your dog, while

    a man on a horse;

is unidentified.

Particles

3.19 *What are Particles?* Particles are small parts of speech. The term **particle** is one used by some 'traditional' grammarians, searching for a predictable pattern in an untidy language, to describe words or parts of words that cannot be fitted into any other group. Not all grammarians use the same term, nor do they all include the same words in the same category. The dictionary defines a particle as a 'relation-word' and as a 'minor part of speech, especially one that is short and indefinable'. Jespersen included conjunctions, prepositions and adverbs in his list – increasing the number of classes into which some words fell and, as a result, increasing our bewilderment.

3.20 Modern grammarians have sought to get over this difficulty of popping words into one box after another by taking their scissors and cutting all words into much smaller parts and renaming them. They then redefine the functions of the parts. In *Grammar* (1971, Pelican) Professor Palmer explains different modern systems of grammatical divisions and the theories behind them for anyone keen enough to dig deeper.

3.21 Having admitted their existence, we must look at the function of particles. They can show direction or place, link parts of a sentence together and qualify. Since the purpose of this book is to make writing good English simpler, we will abandon the scissors-and-tweezers hobby of precise classification and concentrate on those that reverse definition, indicate comparison and change an adjective into a noun or an adverb: *un-, a-, im-, non-, er-, -ness, -ly* and etc. The only particles we concern ourselves with are called **prefixes, suffixes** and **proclitic particles**, those that join themselves to a following word.

3.22 *Magic syllables:* By adding *un-* to *necessary* we make a new word which is exactly opposite in meaning. Although it is a commonplace word it is one that is often mis-spelt, only, I think, because we are unaware of having added a particle. We need never overlook the second *n* in *unnecessary* if we remember the addition. *Mild*, an adjective, becomes a virtuous noun, *mildness*, with a **suffix** or added ending. *Quick* changes to an adverb, *quickly*. If we put *im-* before *partial* the word alters in taking on a **prefix** that means 'against'.

3.23 **Proclitic particles** are those which are 'loosely attached to the following word': *(to)wards, (in)to* and etc. They have the effect of strengthening the sense of direction or position. We can probably also think of those useful words, the **interjections** and **contractions**, as being in this category: *notwithstanding, however, thereafter* and so on.

3.24 As they appear to be largely the product of the grammarians' or philologists' enthusiasm, particles may seem out of place in a simple handbook. But we have to remember not only how to alter a word for meaning, but how that alteration comes about and what manner of word we have formed. *Amoral* and *immoral* have different meanings; *inwards* and *into* are not the same, and *handsomely* is no longer an adjective.

Pronouns
3.25 To avoid repeating nouns over and over again when the reference is obvious, some words act as substitutes, standing in for the nouns. We also need to refer to things without naming them or to ask about something unknown. The code words used in all these cases are pronouns. Like nouns, they can be classified according to the job they do:

Personal pronouns identify us and the people and animals around us:

> I, you, she, he, it;
> we, you, they;
> me, you, her, him, it;
> us, you, them.

Reflexive pronouns are emphatic or particular:
> myself, yourself, herself, himself, itself;
> ourselves, yourselves, themselves.

Possessive pronouns are the sign of ownership:
> my, your, her, his, its;
> mine, yours, hers, his, its;
> our, your, their;
> ours, yours, theirs.

Interrogative pronouns are used in questions;
> who, what, which.

Relative pronouns are substitutes for nouns that are the subjects or objects of clauses:
> who, whom, whose;
> which, what, that.

Demonstrative pronouns are 'pointers':
> this, that, these, those, such, same.

Indefinite pronouns:
> one, some, any, either, all, both, every, an, each.

Negative pronouns:
> none, neither.

Reciprocal pronouns:
> each other, one another.

Recognition and the antecedent

3.26 Pronouns are probably the first words learnt by the English-speaking child. Recognition of self is expressed by *I* and *me*, fundamental words in a two-year-old's vocabulary. The fact that certain verbs are often acquired at the same time is not relevant to this discussion; *I want* and *give me* have probably more to do with Original Sin. Whatever their motives, children easily learn to distinguish between themselves and others in speech by using pronouns in simple sentences.

3.27 Pronouns have kept some of the characteristics of

the ancestral languages and so they have inflections, in common with most European languages. If we speak of 'the doctor', 'the pharmacist' or 'the cat', the listener or reader has no way of knowing whether the people are men or women, or whether the cat is a tom or a queen. Since pronouns are used *instead* of nouns, they must be precise in pointing out somebody or something when we

1. know to whom or to what we refer;
2. have already mentioned someone or something;
3. are asking about someone or something.

They tell us:

which person or thing (person):
    I, me; you; she, her; he, him; it;

whether the person is male or female (gender):
    male: he, him; *female:* she, her; *indeterminate or neuter:* it;

how many (number):
    singular: I, me, she, he;
    plural: we, us, they, them.

3.28 In spite of these definite indications, pronouns in written work must have an antecedent. They can only be used to refer to something that has already been mentioned. In *Disorderly persons* we will look at the muddle that arises from uncertainty about antecedents.

Gender in pronouns
3.29 *He* and *she* are pronouns with unmistakable masculine and feminine antecedents. When they are used the reader can reasonably infer that the noun or name to which one or the other is attached refers to a man or a woman. However there is one group of nouns which pose a problem for the pronoun-user. Nouns in this group refer to occupations or professions which may be followed by either sex. In the 18th century the masculine pronoun served very well as the pursuits of men and women were disparate. Today doctors and nurses, editors and midwives, judges and engineers, solicitors

and barristers, not to mention writers and readers, are just as likely to be women as they are to be men.

3.30 If the reference is to one specific person, known to the writer, the right pronoun is easily found. If a hypothetical person is the antecedent, what pronoun should be used? The word *man* has as one of its fundamental meanings that of a human being regarded in the abstract. In German the noun *man* is impersonal, meaning *one, everyone* or *all people* and we have retained this sense in uses like *mankind* and *man cannot live by bread alone*. It also forms the ending of words like *chairman*, for which *chairperson* is an ugly and awkward substitute.

3.31 Nevertheless, *he* has no abstract or neuter meaning. Third person it may be, but few men would care, I think, to have it regarded as a neuter pronoun; yet to use a specifically masculine or feminine pronoun is not justified when it means ignoring half the expected readership.

3.32 When, as in this book, one is addressing both men and women, there is only one solution. The way to make the reference equal and truly general is to use the plural form of the noun, whenever possible, and refer to a hypothetical group rather than an imaginary individual. It is then in order to use the non-specific pronouns *they, their* and *them*.

Case in pronouns
3.33 Pronouns are among the few English word-forms that change substantially to fit their situation or use. Until you understand **case**, you can never be sure of using pronouns and prepositions properly.

3.34 One reason for muddling the case of pronouns is tidy-mindedness. Because *he, she* and *me* rhyme there is a feeling that they must all represent the same case. To clear up the matter beyond argument, I will list pronouns by person and case:

1. Nominative case – person speaking or initiating action:

    a. First person singular:
       I – I sneeze;
    b. Second person singular:
       you – you sing;
    c. Third person singular:
       he, she, it – he growls;
    d. First person plural:
       we – we sneeze;
    e. Second person plural:
       you – you congregate;
    f. Third person plural:
       they – they interrupt.

2. Accusative case – person receiving or affected by action:

    a. First person singular:
       me – Henry hit me;
    b. Second person singular:
       you – the boss fired you;
    c. Third person singular:
       her, him, it – she loves him;
    d. First person plural:
       us – forgive us;
    e. Second person plural:
       you – Mr Jones is suing you;
    f. Third person plural:
       them – I dislike them.

3.35 If you have never formally studied Latin or any other structured language, you may find it hard to grasp the idea of case. Formal study does not mean learning conversational French while wearing a collar and tie; rather it is the study of a language through its structure and components. People who have had even a year or two of Latin find that the detailed examination of word-forms and their relationships gives them a feeling for case in English even where it is invisible.

3.36 The subject of a sentence, the speaker or prime mover, is always in the **nominative case**. It may be easier to think of it as the **subjective case**. The object of a sentence, the person spoken to or the recipient of action, is always in the **accusative** or **objective case.** Thus in *the cat bit the dog*, the cat is the subject and the dog is the object. If we use pronouns it becomes *she bit him.*

3.37 *Is anyone there?* Before we enter the pronoun minefield, it will be useful to clear one obstacle out of the way. If you go home, having forgotten your key, what do you shout through the letterbox? You may feel obliged to bawl *It is I*, in the belief that *It's me* is bad grammar. The theory behind this widespread notion is that *me*, as the accusative pronoun, is inappropriate after *it is* and that the nominative *I* should be used in such circumstances.

3.38 Nineteenth-century grammarians, ever fond of rigid rules, seem to have taken a firm stand on *It is I.* By the twentieth century the grammarian-mugwump* had decided that it was probably acceptable to use *It is me* in spoken English but that the nominative must be used in the same sentence in written English. C.T. Onions makes a half-hearted attempt to justify *It is I* by referring to an Old English form which translated as *It I am.* He then comes down squarely on top of the fence by saying that *It is me* 'is frequent in current English' and is used by speakers who would regard *It's him* as vulgar or dialectical. Professor Zandvoort describes *It's me* as a 'stressed oblique form' but feels that written English prefers the nominative. With this I have to agree, if only because the constructions used in written English are not the same simple statements except in written dialogue.

3.39 One reason for the disapproval of the spoken form relies on the application of a rule of Latin grammar: the verb *sum* (to be) always takes the nominative 'on both sides'. *He is he* and *I am I* and can never be *he is him* or *I am me.* In French, however, *It is me* has an exact parallel. G.H. Vallins, in *The Pattern of English*, mentions the confusing and contradictory attitudes of different grammarians. Some feel that it is now acceptable because it has been hallowed by usage over a long period of time. Others feel that it can be regarded as a particular construction. How do the French treat it? After

---

*An American animal of uncertain provenance which habitually tries to come down on both sides of the fence at the same time.

the identifying *C'est* (It is) the correct French usage is the disjunctive pronoun *moi* (me). *Moi*, in *C'est moi*, is described as an emphatic nominative which should make it respectable in English eyes.

3.40 The usage could be a survival from the period of Norman dominance, perhaps used by Anglo-Saxon serfs in addressing their Norman lords. But one must be wary, always remembering the difference between spoken and written English. The short reassuring announcement of your presence is the only sentence in which the use of the 'emphatic nominative' can be countenanced. You cannot write *It was me who stole the sausage* and still be among the angels. In the more complex sentences of written English *it was* serves as an introductory verbal phrase; you are really saying *I stole the sausage.* If you turn the sentence about in different ways the cases remain the same: *I it was who stole the sausage.* For the effect of moving from the active voice of the verb to the passive voice, see **4.47–9.**

3.41 *Topsy-turvy:* The most common mistakes, even in written English, involve reversing the case of the pronouns. I suspect that there is a fear that the use of the objective or accusative case in some constructions may sound disrespectful or too informal:

> Uncle Henry took the vicar and I to the opera.

The mistake should, by now, leap to the eye. *I* is a nominative; it must refer to the person initiating the action. Since Uncle Henry produced the tickets and, presumably, paid for them, it seems hard to take the credit from him. To see the extent of the error we take *the vicar* away:

> Uncle Henry took I to the opera.

Not even the vicar can make sense of that. A quick change into the accusative puts it right:

> Uncle Henry took the vicar and me to the opera.

3.42 Inverting the sentence can make the writer's grip on the case of pronouns falter:

> Between you and I there is agreement.

Perhaps the right case makes this statement seem over-familiar. Straightening out the structure of the sentence and making a substitution will clarify matters. In the simple expression:

> You and I agree

you and I are initiators of action and are, correctly, nominative. Now try

> There is agreement between we.

That is obviously absurd. The list under *Case in pronouns* shows *we* as a nominative and the ear tells us that it cannot be right. Using an accusative instead, the sentence settles back into place:

> There is agreement between us.

Even when *us* is divided between the original parties to the agreement, it will still have to be in the accusative:

> Between you and me there is agreement.

3.43 The number of mistakes and confusions over the uses of *you and I, he* and *him* and *she* and *her* suggest that because *you* is the same in both the nominative and accusative, writers tend to believe that the accusatives *me, him* and *her* are merely elegant variations.

> It was her that contacted me.

The writer's best friend is his ear. The sentence above should, if said aloud, sound wrong. If something sounds wrong, then it is necessary to analyse the sentence. Begin by distinguishing between the introductory phrase and the true subject. Abandoning *it was*, the true subject is quite clear:

> She contacted me.

The technical mistakes in the original sentence are (a) a confusion over the true subject and (b) the use of *that* instead of *who*. So we arrive at

> It was she who contacted me.

3.44 *The unseen case:* The dative case is no longer visible in English word-forms. It is the case of the indirect object: something that is indirectly affected by an action expressed by using *to* and *for*:

> He gave a pineapple to her.
> Farnsworth brought cigars for him.

We usually write

> He gave her a pineapple

and

> Farnsworth brought him cigars.

These are simplifications of construction which increase the succinctness and flexibility of English as a written language. Nevertheless, we have to remember the invisible *to* and *for* so that we can keep hold of the real object. In the first sentence *pineapple* and in the second *cigars* are direct objects; *for him* and *to her* are indirect objects and in the dative case. Identifying the indirect object is quite straightforward in simple sentences. In more complex sentences, it is not always so easy. Such sentences can tangle like roots in some hands and the indirect object has to be picked out before the snarl can be undone.

> As you have been so kind about my paintings I should like to come at a time when I can show them you at your convenience.

Who, one wonders, is being shown to what? If the writer felt that he had to leave out the preposition *to* before *you*, it would have been more sensible to reverse the positions of *you* and *them*, when the ambiguity might have been less apparent. It is always better, however, to put the preposition in where there is any possibility of misunderstanding.

. . . when I can show them to you . . .

We shall take a closer look at prepositions later, in Chapter Five.

Possessive pronouns
3.45 Most human beings are acquisitive and possession comes naturally to us. We never make a mistake with the word *my* except when the article in question belongs to someone else and we have possessed it by force or piracy. The genitive, or possessive, case, however, covers all owner-ship and some writers find themselves on uncertain ground when they leave the safety of their own possessions. To make things quite clear here is a list:

1. Simple possessives:
   a. First person singular:
      my – my hat;
   b. Second person singular:
      your – your hat;
   c. Third person singular:
      her, his, its – its hat;
   d. First person plural:
      our – our hats;
   e. Second person plural:
      your – your hats;
   f. Third person plural:
      their – their hats.

2. Double, or absolute, possessives:
   a. First person singular:
      mine – that is mine;
   b. Second person singular:
      yours – that is yours;

c. Third person singular:
hers, his, its – that is hers;
d. First person plural:
ours – those are ours;
e. Second person plural:
yours – those are yours;
f. Third person plural;
theirs – those are theirs.

3.46 Please look carefully at 1.c. and 2.c. You will notice that there is no apostrophe in *its.* Many years ago I worked for an editor who insisted that any manuscript in which the apostrophe in *its* was misplaced should be returned without further reading. He felt that a writer with so little understanding of his own language did not deserve to have his work published. It was a harsh judgement but related to a time when everyone who went to school studied grammar. The difficulty arises because two words spelt in the same way have quite different meanings:

Its without an apostrophe stands for possession or ownership: the cat licks its fur.

It's with an apostrophe is an abbreviation for *it is:* It's a fine day.

If you are really unable to decide whether the *its* you have written deserves an apostrophe, try substituting the word *his*; if the sentence still makes sense, then *its* is a possessive and requires no apostrophe.

3.47 Many people muddle the double, or absolute, possessives: ours, hers, yours and mine, *none of which has an apostrophe* though often awarded an unnecessary one by the over-anxious. The simple possessive is close to the noun:

Where is my coat?

The absolute possessive stands in for the noun, especially where there are two or more possessives in the same sentence:

That is your coat; this is mine.

Mine is an even more useful word when the repetition would be excessive:

I have found her coat and your coat but where is mine?

Before both *coats* only simple possessives are needed. The double possessive *mine* implies *coat* without repeating the word. You could also say:

I have found her coat and yours, but where is mine?

One coat in the sentence is enough.

3.48 Double possessives give trouble in their turn:

This is hers and my birthday.

This sort of sentence is better rephrased at once. If you leave out *and my* you are left with

This is hers birthday.

This is instantly seen as nonsense. The first sentence, although of a kind often heard, is very clumsy because the speaker has tried to economize. It is better not to save words at the expense of sense; rephrase it as either

This is both her birthday and my birthday

or

This is our birthday, hers and mine.

The double possessives *hers* and *mine* in that sentence have *birthday* as the antecedent. The thought would be even better expressed as

She and I share the same birthday.

Disorderly persons

3.49   Personal pronouns, by their nature, refer to people or things that have been, in one way or another, previously identified. In the first and second person there is no reason to indicate the sex of the speaker or the person spoken to; the answer is known or not relevant to the situation. If *you* speak to *me* the implication is that we are both present, or know each other and recognize the gender to which each belongs. We are also aware of the other person's identity in circumstances where gender is of no importance: *I* am writing for *you*, the reader. *We* presents no problem because the speaker is part of a group consisting of *I and you* or *I and they* – all friends, or at least nodding acquaintances, together.

3.50   When third-person pronouns are used, however, the writer must let the reader see the rabbit. If your trail of references is to be followed, it must be clear to whom any third-person pronouns apply. A third-person pronoun needs a noun as an antecedent.

> If a man were to accost the first homely-featured or plain-dressed young woman of his acquaintance, and tell her bluntly, that she was not handsome or rich enough for him, and that he could not marry her, he would deserve to be kicked for his ill manners.
>
> Lamb: *The Behaviour of Married People*

So far, so good. The kickable man and the hard-up grotty young woman are the antecedents for *his*, *him* and *he*, *she* and *her*. Ambiguity can creep in when there is a need to refer to more than one man or woman, boy or girl, in the same sentence.

> During the dissensions in England, Robert Bruce, having pretty well secured Scotland, took a fancy to Ireland too – invaded the country himself, came rather suddenly back again, and sent his brother Edward, who even had the impudence to be crowned King of Ireland; but the English forces coming up with him, took his crown from him with his head in it – and so ended the reign of the Bruces in Ireland.
>
> Thackeray: *Miss Tickletoby's Lectures on English History*

Whose crown? Whose head? As the subject of the sentence is Robert Bruce, readers could be forgiven for wondering if he was the brother whose career ended so suddenly. Muddled personal pronouns can happen anywhere.

> He trusted in God; let him deliver him now, if he will have him; for he said, I am the Son of God.
>
> Matthew xxvii, 43

Third-person pronouns can cause confusion as well.

> And it came to pass that night, that the angel of the Lord went out, and smote in the camp of the Assyrians an hundred fourscore and five thousand: and when they arose early in the morning, behold, they were all dead corpses.
>
> 2 Kings xix, 35

If you read the whole chapter you can deduce that it was the Israelites who arose and not the Assyrian dead. Nevertheless, one is not employing the reader as a detective to ferret out the meaning of anything one has written, and it is fairer to have the antecedent in plain view.

3.51 In giving an account of events, we often feel the need for brevity. In doing so, however, it is too easy to expunge the hallmarks, erasing the identification the reader needs.

> He saw a man coming from an alley on his right. Grasped by his tie, he was shaken to and fro before being flung to the ground. Someone kicked him as he lay there.

Who is the victim? Is it our hero? Or has the man from the alley been mugged, with our hero as horrified onlooker? Some writers of popular fiction can keep up this sort of puzzle for four or five consecutive paragraphs, to the annoyance of the reader. When too many *hes* and *shes* spin off your pen, it is time to rewrite the sentence.

3.52 Some mistakes are due to ordinary carelessness:

> He offered to see her home but it was thrown back in his face.

Perhaps there was an unusually high wind that night. It is more likely that we are to understand that the man is being rejected with contumely. *It* seems to have slid into the sentence. *She* must either throw back his *offer* or *he* must make an *offer*. *It* cannot possibly refer to the verb *offered*. As a pronoun it is indissolubly linked to a noun.

His offer to see her home was thrown back in his face.

Babies, bathtubs, baboons and bananas

3.53   The bathtub was heavy; it slipped from their grasp and thundered down the stairs.

There is no difficulty in understanding here. *It* is plainly the *bathtub*; *bathtub* is the antecedent. Since pronouns must have noun antecedents, we know the antecedents must be identifiable. The gender of the pronoun used is usually a sufficiently accurate pointer, but we can run into problems with the neuter *it*.

3.54 *It* is mostly used for inanimate objects and for animals. It is also used for babies and children when they are unnamed or hypothetical. Jespersen quotes a sentence that is ambiguous but, he feels, unlikely to be misunderstood:

If the baby does not thrive on raw milk, boil it.

There are always people ready to take statements literally. Instructions should never leave any doubt about procedure:

Try using boiled milk if raw milk does not suit the baby.

The baby may suffer indigestion but it will be spared the fate of turnips and cabbage. There is no way of avoiding the use of the same pronoun to refer to children or animals and inanimate objects in the same sentence, when the gender of the child or animal is not known, except by recasting the thought.

The baboon is a wild animal; it dislikes cars driving

through the park and will attack one, snapping off its aerial and pulling at its windscreen wipers.

or

When the toddler is awake and about, watch the boiling pan on the cooker; it can easily pull it over on itself.

Of course we know at once what is meant. But will it be as clear to someone who reads with difficulty, or for whom English is a foreign language? The possible confusion is evident when one reads the instructions on some foreign equipment sold in this country. Translated into English, they are frequently very difficult to understand, even apparently contradictory. If equipment is to be used properly and safely, the writer of instructions has a duty to remove all ambiguities and statements that could be in any way misinterpreted. Precision must be your watchword.

3.55   Apart from the straightforward usage, where a noun is replaced –

a banana is delicious when it is ripe –

the neuter pronoun is widely used in English for other purposes. We use *it* unspecifically:

It's ten o'clock;
Is it a long way?
Fred will catch it when Mother gets home.

In this usage *it* is an idiomatic way of introducing a thought, idea or concept, filling in where words have been left out of a sentence or rephrasing a sentence. We could say *the time is ten o'clock, how far is Babylon* or *Fred will be punished.* C.T. Onions (in *Modern English Syntax*, revised edition, Routledge and Kegan Paul: 1971) calls this a *formal* subject.

It is meet and right so to do;
It is early;
It does not make sense;

> Make a day of it;
> It means trouble;
> He lords it over me.

Extremely personal

3.56 The reflexive pronouns have the effect of emphasis:

> He did it himself.

which is a way of saying that he did it alone, without help. And they act reflexively:

> Shall I help myself?

and

> He distinguished himself on the battlefield.

You are not, in the first instance, offering to act as waiter. The hero, in the second example, won his own medal and not that of anyone else.

3.57 The reflexive pronoun usually has a pronoun for an antecedent, swinging the sense back towards the subject. Compare

> I closed the door when I left.

with

> I closed the door after myself.

In the first sentence the focal point is the door. In the second, the weight of concentration is turned back to *I*, the speaker. The direction of attention, then, is a prime function.

3.58 While reflexive pronouns are capable of being misused, there are occasions when their use is less mistaken than clumsy. The over-formality of

> My troop commander and myself shared the duties

does not sound or look as effective as

My troop commander and I shared the duties.

Substituting a reflexive pronoun where a plain nominative or accusative would fit the sense always makes a tacky sentence:

He has offered to take you and myself in his car.

Unless there is a very particular reason for using *you and me* in such sentences, they are always more harmonious if the accusative plural is used:

He has offered to take us in his car.

3.59 It is an abuse of reflexive pronouns to divide them by another word. One must make a clear distinction here. In

my other self

self is not part of a pronoun but is a noun in its own right. However the often-seen but meaningless compliment which sends wishes 'to your good self' may suggest that you have a *bad* self, which is interesting though hardly flattering. But the expression is a Pooterish Edwardian solecism which has no place in an educated person's vocabulary.

Demonstrative pronouns
3.60 Unnecessary repetition is tedious and distracting for the reader who must plough through the same sequence of words twice in order to find the object of his attention. In matters referring to two groups of things, the writer must often remind the reader of one or the other group. One way of avoiding the tiresome repetition is to use demonstrative pronouns: *this, that, these, those.*

3.61 *That man over there:* The distinction between demonstrative pronouns is one of distance, like that between *here* and *there. This* and *these* are used for things that are close to the writer or speaker, nearer in time or preferred – nearer to his heart. *That* and *those* are further away and often used for things of which the writer takes an objective, considered view. Demonstrative pronouns can be conveniently precise:

> These cabbages look fresher than those cauliflowers.
> This man worked hard; that man did nothing.

However they must either point to something in plain sight or obvious to the reader, or, like other pronouns they must have a clear antecedent.

3.62 Among the most frequent errors in speaking, and not unknown in print, are *these kind of* and *those sort of*. In spite of their occurrence at all educational levels, they are errors of ignorance. The pronouns *these* and *those* refer, in these contexts, to the first noun, not the second; they relate to *kind* or *sort*, not to the objects being classified. Newsreaders plunge in with

> these sort of topics will be discussed . . .

quite forgetting that *topics* have no connection with *these*. Always remember that *these* and *those* are plural and cannot precede a singular noun: *this man*; *these men*. If you refer to a particular type of jam, you write:

> this kind of jam

but if your subject is a group of flavours or recipes, then you write

> these kinds of jam

or

> these kinds of jams

but never, ever,

> these kind of jams.

Relative pronouns

3.63 *Who and Whom:* The distinction between spoken and written English is sharply drawn by the interrogative and relative pronouns. The nominative, or subjective, *who* tends to be used for both nominative and accusative in speech; the accusative, or objective, *whom* is so little used that it strikes the hearer as odd and pedantic. The writer, on the other hand, must be meticulous about case. We may say

Who did you give it to?

without a second thought. When writing, the case is watched carefully.

A list of persons to whom keys have been given . . . ;
The man of whom he wrote . . . .

You will notice that in these sentences *whom* is associated with prepositions. If you are doubtful about a relative pronoun, a useful check is to rephrase the sentence. If the pronoun is naturally preceded by *of, to* or *by* it should be in the accusative.

3.64 Since the cases of pronouns are facts, not fancies, it might be supposed that misjudgement was impossible. Regardless of the evidence, however, it is commonplace to find writers stuffing accusatives into nominative holes, in the belief, perhaps, that *whom* is a more formal and elegant way of saying *who*. Philip Howard, writing in *The Times*, took exception to a sentence that had appeared in *The Times Diary*:

Thomas Huxley had a no less famous son whom (one presumed) was also called Geksli like his father.

Incensed, quite rightly, by the inappropriate use of the accusative *whom* as the subject of a clause, Mr Howard looked at the misuse of cases.

3.65 Using Sir David Hunt as his authority, he has decided that if one or more words, including a verb, appear between the pronoun and the verb of which it is the subject writers may indulge themselves with an accusative. I must say at once that he would not do such a thing himself. He would, however, allow less careful writers more leeway. He therefore regards the next two sentences as permissable:

(1) Mrs Thatcher, whom he said is Prime Minister . . . ;
(2) Mr Tatchell, whom Michael Foot declared would never be a Labour candidate . . . .

I object very strongly to both these sentences. Mr Howard and Sir David are condoning gross errors. Sir David's rule cannot be taken seriously for under it one might say

Whom, tell me, are you, sir?

Mr Howard does not like the rule but does not condemn the writers for their glaring misconstructions. If the sentences had been punctuated, the incorrect cases would have been obvious. When they are rewritten we can see that the nominative is the only possible case.

(1) Mrs Thatcher, who is, he said, Prime Minister . . . ;
(2) Mr Tatchell, who, Michael Foot declared, would never be a Labour candidate . . . .

3.66 A properly used accusative can also be shoved out of the way by fearful writers, especially when it is the first word in a question.

Who do you think the prize should go to?

Since *you* is the subject of the sentence, *who* can hardly be right. The mistake is the result of clumsy phraseology, based on colloquial spoken English. If the preposition *to* and the pronoun are kept together, that sort of mistake cannot happen.

To whom do you think the prize should go?

Lord Radcliffe, in a speech to the House of Lords given on

the 13th December, 1967, said

> Whom have they gone to, if anybody?

He was *speaking*, so the misplaced pronoun is excusable. Nevertheless he has correctly used the accusative *whom*. If he had written the statement, I do not doubt that he would have placed the preposition at the beginning of his sentence.

Rich relatives and poor relations

3.67 Rules and admonitions governing the use of *that* and *which* or *who* have been laid down by a number of grammarians. Briefly, *that* is used to introduce a **defining relative clause** and *which* or *who* to introduce a **non-defining relative clause**. But how shall we know these relative clauses? The names given above are, I think, confusing. The clause described as defining is called by Zandvoort a restrictive clause because it restricts the reference of the antecedent:

> This is the house that Jack built;
> He was a bold man that first ate an oyster.

One can think of it as a clause that is essential to the meaning of the sentence. *The house* to which our attention is directed is the one built by Jack and no other. There are many bold men, but the one that concerns us is the one bold enough to try an unprepossessing mollusc. Let Macaulay give us some more examples:

> At the same time, it must be admitted *that*, in Clive's case, *there were many extenuating circumstances.*
>
> On the contrary, he avowed with the greatest openness *that the Nabob's bounty had raised him to affluence.*

The relative clauses that restrict the reference of the antecedent are shown in italics. In the first sentence there is not a general admission, but a specific admission *that there were many extenuating circumstances.* The second sentence's relative clause restricts what Clive avowed to the effects of the Nabob's bounty.

3.68 The non-defining relative clause tells us something more about the antecedent without disturbing the sense of the whole sentence. It is usually set off from the main part of the sentence by a comma and a stop, or by a pair of commas. Its effect is descriptive but it is not 'restricting'; the rest of the sentence could get along very well without it. It serves to enlarge a description of its own antecedent, not of all objects in the class of the antecedent:

> With Cowper, Hastings formed a friendship *which neither the lapse of time nor a wide dissimilarity of opinions and pursuits could wholly dissolve.*

> The southern part of the Mississippi River, *which constantly changes course,* often floods the surrounding land.

In the first sentence, the relative clause (shown in italic type as before) applies to the *friendship,* describing the indissolubility of the relationship. The basic sentence, straightened out, becomes *Hastings formed a friendship with Cowper.* The information in the clause relates to that friendship only, not to that friendship among others. The next relative clause tells us something that is specific to the Mississippi River; the river is not compared with any other river; if it were not too clumsy, the clause could be replaced by a compound adjective: *constantly course-changing,* inserted before Mississippi.

3.69 Having described these clauses, I have to say that the distinction can be carried too far. If the writer must, when framing a sentence, analyse his thought to see whether he has come up with a defining or non-defining clause, he will waste as much time and effort as if he had decided to pick out one particular kind of seed from a packet of mixed bird-seed. Instead, he must cultivate his ear and develop sensitivity.

3.70 With sense and sound as the guiding principles, let us look at more examples, without worrying about their defining or non-defining nature but rather looking at their meaning:

> I buy cheeses that I like.

The sense is quite clear; I don't buy cheeses that I do not enjoy. However,

> I buy French cheeses, which I prefer.

tells us that I buy a particular sort of cheese and, as it happens, I do so because I prefer them.

> This is the beanstalk that Jack climbed.

We know from this statement that this one special stalk, among all the stalks about us, is the one Jack chose to climb. But

> This is the beanstalk, which Jack climbed to reach the giant's lair.

implies that we are being shown the particular stalk in any case, and that our informant wants to tell us something of its history. The comma is important, because it sets off the descriptive part of the sentence from the rest.

> Alexander was the greatest hero that the ancient world produced.

By now your instinct should tell you that only *that*, never *which*, can be used in the sentence above. And you will also, I hope, see that *which* is necessary in the next sentence:

> The frog sat under the waterspout, which was overflowing.

So much for sense. Sound presents a different problem. If you have a very complex sentence, you may find you have too many *that*s:

> I want you to know that I serve that Department that is responsible for that defence establishment that protects the installation.

A little work on recasting the sentence will make most of them disappear:

> I want you to know that the Department, in which I serve, is responsible for the defence establishment that protects the installation.

Negative pronouns

3.71 *The cancellation factor:* In Macaulay's essay on Warren Hastings there is a sentence which was used as an example in the last section. It is also a good example of the use of negative pronouns:

> With Cowper, Hastings formed a friendship which neither the lapse of time, nor a wide dissimilarity of opinions and pursuits, could wholly dissolve.

When using *neither – nor,* some writers feel that they should add further emphasis by inserting *not* before the verb. Unfortunately this immediately cancels the effect of the pronouns, as you can see:

> . . . *neither* the lapse of time, *nor* a wide dissimilarity . . . , could *not* dissolve.

Reciprocal pronouns

3.72 There is a subtle difference between *each other* and *one another.* There is no hard-and-fast rule that requires the use of either in particular circumstances but the slight shade of meaning can be used for precision when necessary. Although they can usually be regarded as interchangeable, *each other* is more appropriate when there are two persons; in writing of a larger group of people, *one another* is less limiting. In this first example, either pronoun would do:

Nine candidates waited together for the audition, ready
to tear each other's eyes out to get the part.

There is a somewhat more exact sense in:

On the long march, the two men did all they could for
each other.

In

The fortunate candidates congratulated one another.

we infer that there were a number of lucky people. *Each* is
sometimes described as a pronoun of duality.

Adjectives – Image Intensifiers

3.73 Nouns, by themselves, are descriptive in a general
sense. *Refrigerator, elephant* and *budgerigar* are descriptions
of objects in a category. When we need to enlarge the description and to ascribe specific qualities to one or more of the
objects, we use adjectives:

the *old* farm;
the *fat* bookmaker.

Adjectives **qualify** a noun by indicating quality:

a *little* dog.

They also **quantify**:

a *little* milk.

Groups of words, like the relative clauses we examined in the
section under *Relative pronouns*, act in the same way. They
are called adjective clauses, describing or defining some
characteristic of the noun:

Henrietta, *who had a sweet tooth,* browsed on the icing
of the cake.

Personal nouns can be used as adjectives:

> The Bronte sisters;
> The Booker prize;
> The Iberian peninsula.

And so can attributive nouns:

> The Boy Scout movement;
> a five-mile hike;
> a fox-hunting man;

and superlatives:

> my innermost feelings;
> Devil take the hindmost (of us);

and verbal forms:

> a marauding mouse;
> a galloping horse;
> a burnt-out case.

Comparatives

3.74   Unlike the French, who, regrettably, find themselves saying 'more big' and 'more small', English writers have the advantage of many regular comparative forms made by just changing the endings of many adjectives. Strangely enough, there are English writers who do not stop to think and shove in *more* quite unnecessarily.

3.75   The word 'regular', applied to comparative forms, is important. Because English has grown out of a melange of languages not all comparatives have the same advantage. While a girl can be *prettier*, she has to be *more beautiful*. Beautiful is one of the irregular adjectives that do not take the ending *er*. *Little*, for example, has to stand alone; *littler* is used only by babies and we cannot add *more* or *less*. Thus, as a measure of quantity, it becomes *less* and *least*. For comparisons of size we have to fall back on *small*, *smaller* and *smallest*. *Good* is more fortunate; though irregular, it becomes *better* and *best*, in contrast to *bad, worse* and *worst*.

3.76 The irregular forms cause some people much difficulty. BBC weather-forecasters have particular trouble with *less* and *fewer* . They fall into the mistake of saying that we are to have *less showers*. Now it is possible to have *less* sunshine, but not *less* showers, because *less* is a measure of *quantity* or *size*, not a measure of *number*. For example, you can have less money than you had last week, but fewer coins. Think of Fred:

> He ate less cake than Joe; he had fewer slices.

3.77 Comparatives are capable of over-extension:

> less and less

and

> more and more

emphasize the statements in which they are made. The same sort of strong statement can be made by saying

> less than ever

or

> more than ever.

But the whole effect is lost if one phrase is added to the other:

> more and more than ever

throws away the sense of urgency and importance.

Adverbs — Characteristics and Modifications

3.78   If adjectives enlarge the meaning of nouns by qualifying them, adverbs enlarge the meaning of adjectives and verbs by modification, making the description fuller or more accurate:

> A *very* cold day;
> A *gently* soothing touch.

The adverbs *very* and *gently* have nothing to do with *day* or *touch*; they qualify the qualifiers *cold* and *soothing*. Words that modify verbs, describing the action, are also adverbs:

> He drove *furiously*;
> The mouse scampered *quickly*;
> It lay *still*.

Knowing an adverb when you meet one

3.79   Many simple adverbs declare themselves at once by the suffix *ly*. This suffix does not automatically make an adverb. The adverb *contentedly* is formed by adding the suffix. Silly, on the other hand, is an adjective. It is possible, with a certain degree of contortion, to make it into an adverb *sillily*, but this is a word that looks almost as awkward as it sounds. A writer with a keen ear will avoid it, using *foolishly* or *stupidly*, except when there is no possible alternative.

3.80   Adverb-spotting may seem easy, but the English vocabulary is full of words with multiple uses. Some function as adverbs and moonlight as prepositions or adjectives:

> *In* the beginning was the Word: preposition;
> This is the way *in*: adjective;
> He advanced *in* a ponderous way: adverb.

The same adverb qualifies a qualification:

> It was a *wholly* peaceful occasion,

or modifies the action:

The committee was *wholly* caught up in the argument.

Some small and familiar words are hard to identify as adverbs:

> *All* through the night the storm continued;
> The papers were *all* over the place;
> *All* flesh is grass;
> I gave them *all* I had.

3.81 It is plain that the use to which a word is put determines whether it is an adverb or not. The High Wycombe Water Works, H.W.W.W., can be invoked to remind us of the main classes of adverbs:

1. **Manner** = **How** something happened:
   The mouse emerged *suddenly*.

2. **Time** = **When** something happened:
   The mouse was caught *yesterday*.

3. **Place** = **Where** something happened:
   The dead mouse lay *there*.

4. **Interrogation, Reason** and **Purpose** = to **Whom**, to **What** or **Why**:

   Which mouse was caught?
   He trapped it *because* it ate his cheese.

Add to these the adverbs of **Degree** or **Uncertainty**:

> The current runs *too* fast for swimming;
> You are *very* kind;
> She was *rather* severe;
> I am *quite* tired;
> She is *possibly* mistaken;
> The door opened *almost* at once.

These are adverbs that qualify adjectives and other adverbs.

Unclassified adverbs

3.82   Continential grammarians with neat habits have done their best to classify English adverbs. Like so many other parts of the language, adverbs have defied them. It is like trying to put an octopus into a Babygro; however well some bits fit in, other quite substantial parts have nowhere to go. Here are some of the familiar adverbs that will not fit in:

> Curiously *enough*, I am a mouse fancier;
> I am *certainly* against traps;
> Take a mouthful of cheese *twice* a day;
> The trap was *therefore* laid;
> What art can wash her guilt *away*?

Better and better in every way

3.83   We have already looked at the function of *less* as an adjective of comparison. It is, of course, also an adverb. In

> A less impressive speech,

less qualifies the adjective *impressive* and changes into an adverb. Many adverbs are themselves modified in their comparative state by adding *more* or *most, less* or *least*:

> He works less efficiently.

Those adverbs that have their own comparative forms are also adjectives: faster, harder, and so on.

Position and misposition

3.84   The relationship of the adverb to the verb or adjective is essential. When the adverb is qualifying an adjective it has a place immediately before the word it qualifies:

> An extremely successful meeting.

3.85   When the adverb modifies a verb it usually follows a **finite** or **intransitive verb**, one without an object (**4.12, 4.45–6**):

The floodwaters rose steadily.

But there are times when a complex thought or a change of emphasis can place the adverb at the end of the sentence or before the verb:

He handled the tools deftly;
She steadfastly refused to retract.

While *deftly* relates to *handled*, it has to follow the object of *handled*: *tools*. By placing *steadfastly* before the verb we understand that it modifies the whole way in which she answered, not just her obstinacy.

3.86 Certain familiar phrases tend to fix the adverb in a position away from its verb:

I simply don't care;
Fortunately I won;
He hardly believed it;
I merely said it was a lie;
He only hit me once.

The writer must distinguish between the idiom, which is established by custom, and the catch-phrase, which is ephemeral. An example in current use is:

we stand idly by.

One is tempted to ask 'Stand idly by what?' It is an inversion of

we stand by idly.

In other words we do nothing while watching something happen. But the first sentence, much in vogue with politicians and journalists, means that we are lounging about in some place unspecified. The unfortunate preposition *by* hangs off the end of the sentence in a meaningless way. The verb, after all, is *to stand by*, as a bystander, not *to stand* beside something.

3.87   The same stricture cannot be applied to the following sentence, which would be more awkward if the adverb were placed immediately after the verb:

We often come here in the summer.

3.88   People often forget that adjectives and adverbs need something to qualify or modify. If the right reference is left out, they will attach themselves to any other noun or verb in the sentence. In reporting the result of an attack by armed men in Ireland, a BBC newsreader told us that the attackers had been shot and taken to hospital 'where one is said to be critical'. We could have supposed from that last phrase that the man criticized either the fact of his admission or the way in which the hospital was run. *The Times*, reporting the same incident, said:

The four shot men . . . were taken to hospital . . . and one who was more seriously injured was later transferred to Dublin. The condition of the three others was said to be serious but stable.

The newsreader's statement is a classic example of a wrongly-used adjective attaching itself to the wrong antecedent. *Critical*, an adjective looking for a noun, can only refer to *he* and takes on its non-medical meaning of *fault-finding*. To make sense the statement should have ended:

where one is said to be critically ill.

The Times got it right. *Stable* (or *critical*) attached to condition tells us that the men were seriously wounded. The writer must never forget the distinction between adjectives and adverbs and needs to ensure that the right word has been chosen and the right relationship established.

Adjective and adverb clauses
3.89   Words grouped into a clause can behave in the same way as an adverb, expressing manner, time, place, cause and all the other adverbial functions:

I scatter crumbs *as I eat*;
There I couch *where owls do cry*;
The dog pants *because he is hot*;
He tamed the mouse *in spite of its ferocity*;
If it rains I shall put on my hat;
What is she, *that all our swains adore her*?
The dog chases the cat *although he knows it is wrong*;
It attacked so swiftly *that I could not save myself*.

In the last sentence the clause is related to *so* which qualifies *swiftly*, describing how swiftly.

3.90　Clauses, both adverbial and adjectival, are groups of words which, like mini-sentences, have their own verb but are unable to stand alone because the words form one descriptive or modifying idea. The clauses above explain how, when, where and why things happen. The adjective clause, on the other hand, defines something by giving it a particular attribute. The same sentence can be turned around to make both adverbial and adjectival clauses:

> There is a fish-and-chip shop on the corner. It smells of burnt fat.

First it can be given an adverbial clause of place:

> The fish-and-chip shop, *which is on the corner*, smells of burnt fat.

Next the thought can be turned round to produce an adjectival clause, giving an attribute:

> The fish-and-chip shop, *smelling of burnt fat*, is on the corner.

Chapter Four
Action, state and time

4.1 We live in a world of ceaseless movement. The smallest divisible parts of matter are constantly in motion. We also have an inherent sense of time and period, taking for granted that things happened yesterday or ten years ago, that we are part of events taking place now or that things will come to pass in the distant future or tomorrow. Equally, we are aware that there is a difference between active and inactive things and ideas, and that there are different sorts of activity. A tree is firmly rooted in the ground, but its roots continually take in water, sending it twenty to sixty feet above the ground to the leaves, which transpire at changing rates according to the weather and the time of day.

4.2 Obviously the words which we use to describe and depict things cannot also place events in time, tell us what type of action occurs or what state exists. The part of speech that has the function of indicating action, state and time is the verb. The verb is flexible because it must be capable of carrying out these functions in any statement. The derivation shows its syntactical importance. It comes from the Latin *verbum*: word; noun, which derives from *nomen*, merely means a name.

4.3 The verb charges the sentence with meaning. Nouns the namers of names, are the static part of language; inert, whatever their meaning may be. They may gather particles and adjectives, but they are lifeless until given momentum by a verb. *A javelin* and *an antheap* are equally immobile until the javelin is *thrown*. Even if the statement is only that *a javelin is a projectile*, the noun, *javelin*, has come to life.

4.4 Written English refuses to be tidied away according to a neat and obvious system. The great Dutch and Danish grammarians have done their best but no one has been able to draw neat boundaries around verbs and their uses to make firm rules for the behaviour of all verbs and verbal forms that appear to fall into particular categories. Linguistics attempts to do so by abandoning the familiar grammar of structured European languages. Words are segmented and thought processes split up in an effort to give us new terms to describe the ways in which we express things. It is all good fun, providing endless scope for academic argument and speculation, but it is of little comfort to the writer of a thesis or a company report.

4.5 To categorize nouns, and the words that represent, qualify or modify them according to their function is relatively easy. It is more difficult to do so to verbs. The reduction in inflected forms means that we use the same form in different contexts. We also combine verbal forms to extend meaning. The various sources from which the language derives have each contributed constructions that are idiomatic rather than part of a clear pattern.

4.6 The elaborately inflected Latin verbs made some distinctions very straightforward. The Roman writer could, with a single word, distinguish the person of the speaker, when he spoke, whether he was in the act of speaking at a particular time in the past or whether he was intending to speak. To replace many of the inflections, English has brought the auxiliary verbs into play to a much greater degree. While we use auxiliary verbs with unconscious ease, they still pose problems for the writer. As adults we think in clauses, phrases and sentences without effort. The gulf between the spoken and written languages is widened and the writer who habitually uses the same word patterns can be in trouble. The reader cannot be trusted to unravel the thoughts as easily as they were formed. The writer's task is to communicate with such accuracy that there can be no misunderstanding. The ear, or sense with which we evaluate written work, must be trained to discriminate between the changes in meaning and emphasis carried by different forms and structures, however small the difference.

4.7 Verbs are versatile. A noun cannot act as a verb. It can be used to form a verb but it then becomes wholly a verb and no longer acts as a noun. Its function is definite and limited

79

and it cannot be used alone except in answer to a spoken question:

> What would you like for supper?
> Sausages.

That single word, when written, is obviously unsupported, a form of shorthand. When we hear it, we hear the supporting sentence around it:

> I should like to have sausages for supper.

Written English demands that the supporting words shall be set down.

4.8   Verbs seem more capable of standing alone. On the beach, Uncle sends children running with *Ready! Steady! Go!* while the chap tied to the post hears the officer in charge of the execution shout *Fire!* This use of a single verb is not confined to speech. Mandatory notices on the road command us to *Slow* or *Stop.* A verb is acting in a special manner when it is used alone; and, as this is one of a number of functions a verb can perform, we distinguish this manner as the **imperative mood.**

4.9   Many writers mishandle verbs. To understand the part they play in the process of communication, it is useful to know what can be expected from any part of a verb. The form used in a particular instance must tell us a number of things:

1. whether it refers to one person or thing or a number of persons or things – **number**;

2. whether it refers to the writer or another person or thing – **person**:

> I snivel – 1st person singular
> you snivel – 2nd person singular
> he, she, it snivels – 3rd person singular
> we snivel – 1st person plural

you snivel – 2nd person plural
they snivel – 3rd person plural;

3. the time at which the action takes or has taken place – **tense**, which can be past, present or future: I was, I am, I will be;

4. the manner in which the action takes place – **mood**:

He brought a gin and tonic = **indicative mood** because it states a fact;

Bring me a gin and tonic = **imperative mood** because it is an order;

If he were to bring me a gin and tonic I should be grateful = wishful thinking falls into the **subjunctive mood**;

5. whether the action is carried over to someone or something else – **transition**:

I run a bookshop = **transitive verb** because it has an object;

I run = **intransitive verb** because it does not need an object to complete the sentence;

6. whether the action is carried out by someone or something or happens to someone or something – **voice**:

Al Capone killed his rivals = **active voice**;

Rival gangsters were killed by Al Capone = **passive voice**.

The Principal Parts
4.10   The working verb has a number of basic components, otherwise known as the principal parts:

1. the **infinitive**: to steal;
2. the **present tense**: steal;
3. the **past tense**: stole;
4. the **present participle**: stealing;
5. the **past participle**: stolen.

These parts will, with the addition of nouns, pronouns, prepositions and auxiliary verbs as required, perform all the functions listed in **4.9**.

Finite and non-finite forms
4.11   Although the principal parts of the verb are listed together, they do not all carry the same specific indications of action. They fall into two groups: finite and non-finite forms.

4.12   *Finite forms*: The finite forms are those which place the action within boundaries and carry certain precise indications: the present tense and the past tense. They always have a subject (even when the subject is only implied as it is in the **imperative mood** – **4.37–8**) so they relate to **number**, singular or plural, and **person**, first, second or third.

I invest in property;
The boys stole chestnuts.

They are also precise about time. I am investing now, not last year or next week. The boys have already stolen the chestnuts. In the next example there are two finite verb-forms: one in the present tense and one in the past tense.

Granny scolds because Harold and Myrtle fidgeted during the sermon.

4.13   *Non-finite forms*: The other three parts are non-finite because they do not, in themselves, carry the same positive indications. They are used, with auxiliary verbs, in forming tenses and, as noun-equivalents, adverb-equivalents and adjective-equivalents, when they are related to the subject and time of action through the main verb in the sentence.

It is not sweet with nimble feet
To dance upon the air
                Oscar Wilde: *The Ballad of Reading Gaol*

The infinitive is used here to assist in making a general statement. *To dance* (*upon the air*) is acting as a noun, the subject of *It is not sweet.* What isn't *sweet*? A noun like *vinegar* might be the answer; in this case, *to dance* finishes the statement. In

Let him go, let him tarry

go and *tarry* are infinitives. The infinitive is usually shown with *to* before it in lists of principal parts: *to buy; to sleep; to write.* Many verbs, however, are used with the *to* left out of the infinitive form. We say

I saw him kick the cat,

not

I saw him to kick the cat

any more than, in modern English, we would say

Jones vowed he would make Sackbut to apologize.

4.14 In

1. Many cars are *stolen* every day;
2. *Stolen* plants always thrive;
3. A *stolen* watch will never keep time.

the same past participle can be used in three different statements. It is used with the auxiliary verb *are* (which sets the time in the present) in 1 to tell us what happens to many cars. In 2 and 3 we see that the same form of the verb can be used, regardless of time, person and number and in different contexts, as an adjective. The present participle is just as accommodating.

1. *Skating* is good exercise;
2. He fell heavily while *skating*;
3. I have been *skating*;

In 1, the word *skating* is a noun-equivalent (see **4.26**) and is the subject of the sentence. In 2 the present participle is an adverb describing when the subject *fell*. The same present participle is used in 3 to make a tense which denotes a period of time it cannot state by itself, as it always needs to take its time-significance from auxiliary verbs.

The Infinitive
4.15   There are five main uses of the infinitive.

1. It is used as the name of the verb, its identifying code. It is a reference, so to make it plain that it is not acting as a verb in the sentence it is usually set in italics:

    Harassment is a noun formed from the verb *to harass*.

2. It can act adjectivally:

    I was given a paper to read;
    There is work to do.

3. It can be used as a noun:

    To read in bed is one of life's pleasures;
    To know her is to dislike her.

4. It can be used as an adverb, after an intransitive verb, when it is known as an infinitive of purpose:

    I come to bury Caesar;
    I am waiting to hear your answer.

5. It can be added to another verb, using it as an auxiliary:

    I long to go;
    He wants to work.

It never loses its verbal identity. If we had said

He wants work

we would have used a noun, *work*, not the infinitive.

4.16 The proclitic particle *to* is not always present; the infinitive can be used without it: I would rather die (to die); he need not come (to come). Its use carries a degree of meaning that is implied rather than stated. In the first of the two sentences below the past tense, (*she*) *sang*, tells us only that Miss X changed her mind. The second sentence, using the infinitive *sing* after *she did*, is more emphatic and has an element of surprise or astonishment at her change of heart.

1. Although Miss X had said she would not take part, later she sang one song;

2. Although Miss X had said she would not take part, later she did sing one song.

4.17 *A phantom fiend*: It is widely believed that to split an infinitive is the ultimate solecism. Some people tie sentences in knots lest they should break the rule. Yet many of these writers would not recognize an infinitive even if it bit them savagely on the nose and regard all compound forms of verbs as untouchable.

4.18 The 'crime' is the placing of any word, usually an adverb, between the particle *to* and the verb, which together make up the infinitive form, as in

to horribly scowl.

In the following sentence the infinitive is *to be*, not *supported*, but the writer played safe:

the proposal was put forward as one to be supported generally.

Splitting the infinitive could only have been accomplished by inserting the adverb into *to be*:

> The proposal was put forward as one to generally be supported.

That looks and sounds so unpleasant that there is no excuse for it. To improve both the sound and the sense, the adverb is placed where it belongs: after the infinitive and before the past participle.

4.19   It is nonsense to believe that it is always wrong to insert an adverb into an infinitive. The meaning and the flow of the sentence are what really matter. If you are at all uncertain about the modification please put the adverb in *after*, and not *before*, the infinitive. There is no academic flavour (for that is what the writer seems to be trying to achieve) in a statement like

> I intend clearly to demonstrate . . .

which may show the reader what care has been taken but looks pedantic and fails to convey the unequivocal demonstration that the reader should understand. It is better *to clearly demonstrate* than to show such a lack of courage. The adverb can, in that instance, be placed after the object:

> I intend to demonstrate the truth of the case clearly.

4.20   There are times when the split infinitive will put meaning across better than any 'correct' construction.

> The Member rose emphatically to deny . . .

Did he sit on a pin? Was he wearing pneumatic trousers?

> The Member rose to deny emphatically . . .

That is a weak statement. His heart is obviously not in it. But when

> The Member rose to emphatically deny . . .

we know that it is a very strong denial, not just a mannerism.

4.21 Where emphasis and clarity are as well served by either form, the split infinitive can be avoided. Wilfred Whitten, writing as 'John O'London' in *Is It Good English and Like Matters* (Newnes), points out that a clause like

to considerably improve the present wages

can without any loss of clarity, rhythm or meaning, be written as

to improve the present wages considerably.

My advice is that if, and only if, it improves and strengthens what you want to say, split your infinitive with impunity; if to do so makes your sentence ugly, inharmonious or awkward, keep the infinitive intact.

Participles
4.22 Participles function as verbal adjectives in a number of ways.

1. They are used, with auxiliary verbs, to form compound tenses:

he is waiting; they have shown.

Whether the present or past participle is used is a matter of time: present, elapsed or continuous. There is another sense in which participles do not relate to specific time. In this sense there is a clear difference between the use of the past and present participles. The present participle is *active*; it represents something done or performed by the subject. The past participle is opposite in effect; it is something that happens to the subject and is *passive*. The Rural Dean who announces that he has taken up wife-beating is *shocking.*When he sticks his finger into the light socket, he is *shocked.* The child doing his home work was *studying*; but when he met the educational psychologist he was *studied.*

2. They are used as simple adjectives:

> a *dead* duck; a *dying* swan.

They differ from ordinary adjectives in imparting a sense of time; the cause of, or reason for, the description has already occurred or is occurring. A pretty bird cannot be said, from its adjective alone, to exist in the past, present or future, but a dead duck died before the sentence was written. There is a close tie between the verbal adjectival use and the simple adjectival use. In the first the participle describes what the subject of the auxiliary verb is doing in much the same way that an adjective would qualify the noun:

> the *dead* duck; the duck that was *dead*.

3. They are used attributively:

> the *hanging* judge; the *racing* driver; the *singing* bird.

The participles characterize someone or something by an activity.

4. They act assertively:

> he came in *fuming*; they stood *quarrelling*.

5. They form the basis of adjective phrases:

> Large and smoky red, the sun's cold disk drops,
> *Clipped by naked hills*, on violet shaded snow.
> > George Meredith: *Love in the Valley*

Like a simple adjective, the adjective phrase qualifies a noun. Here *disk* is *clipped by naked hills*. The phrase can be separated from the words it qualifies only if the subject is immediately recognizable.

> Yet was she seen again on many a day,
> By some half-waking mariner or herd,
> *Playing amid the ripples of the bay*.
> > William Morris: *The Earthly Paradise*

4.23 *The dangling participle*: A participle cannot manage to stand alone, unsupported. It must always form part of a verbal construction or qualify a noun, either as one word or part of a phrase.

> Kicking and screaming, the baby was carried from the room.

It is fatally easy, when there is a rush of words to the pen, to overlook the word that supports the participle. Unsupported, the participle will hunt for a subject, even if it finds one the writer did not intend.

4.24 Haste and enthusiasm can lead one astray.

> Writing with a sense of urgency, the letter was soon finished and posted.

A sentence of this sort often creeps into a paragraph in which the subject and the reason for action have already been introduced. However, the fact that the reader may understand what the sentence is meant to convey does not give the writer licence to write nonsense. The *letter* cannot write itself, but the unfortunate participle has to rely on it as the subject of the sentence. This sort of mistake can be corrected by changing the present participle into a past participle. Remember that the present participle has to apply to something that performs the action; the past participle records what happens to the subject (**4.22**):

> Written with a sense of urgency, the letter was soon finished and posted.

More obvious is the totally unattached participle. In the next example the participle has nothing to do with *the little chapel*; the subject has been carelessly left in a previous sentence:

> Continuing your journey through the valley, the little chapel in the village is worth a special visit.

The participle is probably meant to give a feeling of movement, an impression that the writer is travelling with the
reader. The intention is wasted because the reader will sense
that something is wrong and grope for the missing subject. It
is always better to abandon the participle when it does not
fulfil your purpose and recast the sentence as:

> As you continue your journey through the valley, you
> will find that the little chapel in the village is worth a
> special visit.

4.25 Sometimes an unnecessary word can alter the sense of
a participle. In unguarded moments, superfluous *ands* or
thoughs can slip in. W.H. Prescott seems to have had a habit
of pausing for thought halfway through a sentence. During
the pause, he would write *and* before completing the train
of ideas. The conjunction pushed the adjective clause too far
out for safety, making matters worse:

> Repeatedly they saw structures of stone and plaster and
> occasionally showing architectural skill in the execution,
> if not the elegance of design.
>
> W.H. Prescott: *History of the Conquest of Peru*

What confusion! There is nothing wrong with either the
thought or the language; only the construction is faulty. The
phrase *occasionally showing architectural skill* appears to
belong to the subject *they saw* because of the intrusive *and*.
The reader's problem is increased because the main sentence,
they saw structures is introduced by an adverb whose meaning, like that of *occasionally*, relates to something that happens more than once. The sentence can be much improved by
punctuation:

> Repeatedly they saw structures of stone and plaster,
> occasionally showing architectural skill in the execution,
> if not the elegance, of design.

But it would have been better still if rephrased:

> They often saw structures ... which showed architec-
> tural skill ...

Gerunds

4.26 The gerund is a noun made from a transitive verb which can therefore take an object. It ends in *-ing*, like a participle, but its use in sentences is quite different. The participle is a *verbal adjective*, but the gerund, for the purpose of the sentence, is a *verbal noun*. For this reason there are certain conventions to be observed when using it.

4.27 We put together sentences with gerundial subjects all the time without conscious effort.

Digging for treasure is a waste of time.

Digging is the subject, as an ordinary noun might be, but with one difference: it has an object, *for treasure*. The sentence falls naturally into two parts like any other simple sentence: the subject, consisting of the gerund and its object,

Digging for treasure,

and the predicate, which consists of the verb and its object,

is a waste of time.

4.28 Gerunds are often used in adverbial phrases.

The English fleet dispelled all danger of invasion by crossing the Channel, by capturing a number of French ships and by burning Dieppe.
J.R. Green: *A Short History of the English People*

This sentence illustrates something important about the gerund. It is distinguished from the participle, not by its appearance, but rather by *the use to which it is put.* We can see that *crossing, capturing* and *burning* are gerunds because they are preceded by the preposition *by.* Green could, for example, have said *by the capture of a number of French ships,* using an ordinary noun instead of a verbal noun. He could have used participles in that sentence; if we take out the prepositions and place a comma after *invasion*, we can see what effect it has on the statement.

> The English fleet dispelled all danger of invasion, crossing the Channel, capturing a number of French ships and burning Dieppe.

The sentence now describes what the fleet was doing when it dispelled the invasion, rather than describing the means by which the invasion was dispelled. The participle or participial phrase is tangential to the main statement:

> *Churning the milk*, she made butter,

while the gerund forms an essential part of it:

> The churning of milk bringeth forth butter; the wringing of the nose bringeth forth blood.

The wobbly gerund or fused participle

4.29 Remembering the noun character of gerunds is important when we write. If, when speaking, we say

> I don't mind you doing it,

the pronoun passes without comment. But, because the gerund must be treated like any other noun, *when writing it must be preceded by a possessive*.

> There is little hope of the *patient's* recovering.

And this constraint applies to pronouns.

> *His* wearing his hat back to front annoys me

never

> *Him* wearing his hat . . .

The mistake occurs because the writer tries to 'fuse' the gerund with the preceding word and treat it as a participle.

> The Committee passing the amendment pleased the Board.

The Committee didn't please the Board. It was their action that did so.

> The Committee's passing the amendment pleased the Board.

4.30 There are two other parts of the verb that can serve the same purpose: the infinitive and the present tense. To have different ways of making the same sort of statement allows you to vary the texture of your work.

> Infinitive: To err is human, to forgive divine.
> Present tense: Humans err; God forgives.
> Gerund: Erring is human, forgiving divine.

Joos (in *The English Verb*, University of Wisconsin Press, 1964) points out that children begin by using gerunds and progress to using infinitives. Certainly gerunds make rather clumsy constructions and too many gerunds make an indigestible text. Use them sparingly, remembering that there are almost always other ways of phrasing your sentence.

Person and Number
4.31 Like pronouns, verbs are inflected to show which person or thing is engaged in the action. Changes in form are very slight, almost negligible, **Singular and plural forms,** nevertheless, however disguised or imperceptible the difference may be, **must match the number of persons or things involved.**

4.32 Usually any change occurs in the third person singular, which is given a suffix -*s* or -*es*:

> I do; you do; he does;
> we do; you do; they do.

There are exceptions, notably the verb *to be*:

> I am; you are; he is;
> we are; you are; they are.

We usually apply these changes instinctively in speaking, so it ought not to be necessary to mention it. Yet many writers abuse the familiar process. A man who knows very well how many beers he drank when he comes to pay his due often seems unable to see the indissoluble link between the number and person of the subject and the verb form he chooses and will, on paper, unblushingly attach a plural verb to a singular subject in the third person:

> The spacecraft sub-systems *whose proper operation are essential* to the mission are described in the previous article.

The subject of the clause beginning with *whose* is *operation*, a singular noun by any standard. If the clause had been set off with commas, as it should have been, the blunder would have been obvious and he would have changed it to *whose proper operation is essential*. There is one exception to this pattern of agreement. When a third person pronoun is added to a first or second person pronoun, the verb agrees with the first or second person, never the third:

> Do you and he ride today?
> You and Bloggs and I go forward at the same time.

4.33 Two nouns joined by *and* make a plural subject. The writer of the next sentence overlooked this point and mismatched the verb:

> *Morphogenesis and differentiation* of the murine mammary gland *is* dependent on the interaction of peptide and steroid hormones.

Morphogenesis and *differentiation are* dependent, of course. The mistake occurs because the writer attaches the verb to the closest noun, forgetting to include the other elements of a multiple subject.

> Cake, buns, biscuits, trifle and a large red jelly was on the table.

Was it? Where *were* the other foodstuffs? Sometimes people err on the side of safety, clutching at a plural verb after an inserted phrase.

> The large existing building, with the hayloft, stables and coach-house, offer plenty of space.

Unlike the clause in the earlier example (**4.32**), the interpolation here is a phrase without a verb of its own, *with the hayloft, stables and coach-house,* and the writer has borrowed the verb from the main clause to make up the deficiency. Nevertheless, the main clause is quite straightforward and its subject is singular:

> The large building offers plenty of space.

Tense

4.34   Tenses express performance or action at a particular time; the action or state may be finished or continuing. It can also be shown as probable, possible or dependent on circumstances by using the conditional tenses. Because there is a greater emphasis on teaching foreign languages as they are spoken, many people will never have seen a verb system formally set out as a list of named tenses. Although the old method of learning the structure of a language has been abandoned, it is still useful to be able to identify the tense you are employing in a particular instance. Here is a tabulation based on the time and type of action:

1. Present
   a. simple (or perfect): I wait for the bus;
   b. continuous (or imperfect): I am waiting for the bus;
2. Future
   a. simple: I will wait for you;
   b. continuous: I will be waiting for you;
   c. conditional: I would wait for you;
3. Past
   a. simple: I waited for the chairman;
   b. continuous: I was waiting for the verdict;
4. Perfect – action originating in the past but completed at the present time

      a. simple past-in-present: I have waited until now;
      b. continuous past-in-present: I have been waiting since
         noon;
    5. Pluperfect – action in the past that began before the
      time of the statement
      a. simple: I had waited for the verdict;
      b. continuous: I had been waiting for some time;
    6. Future-in-the-Past
      a. simple: I should have waited for him;
      b. continuous: I would have been waiting still if he had
         not come.

The tenses listed above are those which are in general everyday use. Some are more formal and more often seen in
written English but all will be familiar. One that is less often
used should be added to the list although its use is limited:
the Historic Present, which is the Present Tense used instead
of the Past to give a lively and vivid effect to an account:

> At this moment an old clothes-man passes and his deep
> harsh tones sound like an intended insult on one's
> distress and banish the thought of asking for his assist-
> ance, as one's eye glances furtively at an old hat or a
> great-coat hung up behind the closet door. One hesitates
> and the opportunity is gone by; for without one's
> breakfast one has not the resolution to do anything.
>
>   Hazlitt: *Want of Money*

Used widely by writers of fiction in this century to give the
impression of a narrator recalling a sequence of events, it is
of dubious value. An entire novel written in the Historic
Present can be enervating to read; to keep up the level of
immediacy is very tiring. The Present Tense is often found in
descriptions of processes or activities and is particularly
useful in explanations as this clear example shows:

> The ear consists of a drum, a thin membrane stretched
> across an oval opening in the insect's outer skin or
> cuticle. Inside is a group of sensory cells, known as the
> chordatonal organ, and a nerve runs from this to the
> brain.
> Maurice Burton: *Animal Senses*, Routledge and Kegan
> Paul, 1961

4.35 *Keeping an eye on the time*: The main clause in a sentence determines the period of time in which the statement takes, or is taking, place: past, present or future. In compound or complex sentences the tenses in clauses must bear a sensible relationship to the main verb. Sections on the subjunctive and auxiliary verbs will have more detail about idiomatic usage, but this is the point at which writers must remind themselves of the basic sequence of tenses. If we begin *Did he become violent*, and we wish to enlarge on this, we could say *when the moon was full*? and make sense. What we cannot do, without confusing the reader, is to say *Did he become violent when the moon is full*? It is self-evident that when the sentence is set in a particular period of time, all verbs used must relate to that time. If there are two periods of time, the relationship must be watched even more carefully, whatever the position of clauses may be:

> Mrs Smith *had despaired* of seeing her, but she *came* just in time;

> The prisoner *would have died* if he *had* not *come*;

> Fred *was* still *waiting* when Charlie *drove* past;

> I *shall go* to the warehouse now that you *have come*.

Difficulties may arise when there are phrases and interjections interposed between the main clause and subordinate clauses; it is not unknown for writers to forget the precise time indicated by the main verb.

4.36 There is an exception to this sequence. If the subordinate clause makes a permanent, ongoing or universal statement while the main clause deals with a situation in the past, the tenses need not agree:

> The dietician *explained* that boiling sugar *forms* a coarse thread in cold water when it has reached a temperature between 230 and 234 °F,

and

> The guide *told* us that Anakrakatoa *is* an active volcano.

Mood

4.37   Mood is the most elusive of categories. It is defined in the Shorter Oxford English Dictionary as 'Any one of the groups of forms in the conjugation of a verb which serve to indicate the function in which the verb is used.' The definition is correct but does not help us very much; it is intended to apply generally to verbs in all languages. It is easier to think of mood as defining the *type* of action. Although there are four moods in English, we need only pay close attention to the **imperative, optative** and **subjunctive** moods. It follows that everything else falls into the **indicative** mood.

4.38   The imperative mood is addressed to the *second person*, either singular or plural. It can be a direct command to an identified person,

> Go to your room!

or an exhortation to a general group:

> Praise the Lord;
>
> Greet the new day;
>
> Mind the gap;
>
> Reduce speed now.

4.39   The imperative mood has a limited application in a written text and its more frequent colloquial use tends to blur our understanding of it. It is a mood of direct address; the subject is not indicated, even by a pronoun, because the subject is the person addressed. Naturally any word appearing before the verb is not part of the sentence unless it is part of an introductory statement:

> I say to you 'Do it!'

or an adverb modifying the verb:

> Never pick up a snake.

A recent correspondence in *The Times* called attention to the lack of punctuation in warning signs.

LAMBS DRIVE SLOWLY

GIVE WAY MARKINGS ERASED

LOOSE CHIPPINGS SLOW

As these signs are not meant to entertain but to inform us, the imperative sentence should be set off clearly. Full stops after *lambs, give way* and *loose chippings* are needed. When any admonition, warning or instruction is written in the imperative mood, it must deliver its message without any possible ambiguity.

The subjunctive mood
4.40   The subjunctive comes closest to the usual definition of 'mood': a state of mind or expression of feeling, because it is associated with wishing, hoping, desiring:

I would be so happy if I won the Pools.

It is found in subordinate clauses expressing condition:

If I were to die tonight . . .

and purpose:

Lest we forget,

and concession:

Yet though I die, yet shall I live.

4.41   It can be found in main clauses, beginning with *if*, in the future:

If I should ever by chance grow rich
I'll buy Codham, Cockridden and Childerditch,
Roses, Pyrgo and Lapwater,
And let them all to my elder daughter.
　　　　　　　Edward Thomas: *If I Should Ever by Chance*

the present:

> If wishes were horses, then beggars would ride,

and in the past:

> We should not think it necessary to offer any remarks for the purpose of directing the judgement of our readers . . . had not Sir John Malcolm undertaken to defend it in all its parts.
>
> Macaulay: *Essay on Lord Clive*

The last example shows how the subjunctive hides away in idiomatic usage. *We should not think* conceals *should not have thought*; the last part of the sentence is an *if*-clause even though the word does not appear. If it had been worded differently, it would have read *if Sir John Malcolm had not undertaken*.

4.42 The important point about the subjunctive *if*-clauses is their indication of doubt or possibility rather than reality or tangibility. This cannot be better illustrated than by the following poem:

> If there were, oh! an Hellespont of cream
> Between us (milk-white mistress), I would swim
> To you, to show to both my love's extreme,
> Leander-like – yea, dive from brim to brim.
> But met I with a buttered pippin-pie
> Floating upon't, that would I make my boat
> To waft me to you without jeopardy,
> Though sea-sick I might be while it did float.
> Yet if a storm should rise (by night or day)
> Of sugar-snows and hail of care-a-aways,
> Then, if I found a pancake in my way,
> It (like a plank) should bring me to your kays;
>   Which having found, if they tobacco kept,
>   The smoke should dry me well before I slept.
>   John Davies: *Buttered Pippin-pies*

4.43 The tenses used in the subjunctive reflect its conjectural, suppositious character: *should, would, might* and *were* are the auxiliaries most often associated with it. Writers should take notice of the use of *were* in the present subjunctive.

> If it were done when 'tis done, then 'twere well done quickly.
>
> Shakespeare: Macbeth

A more up-to-date example would be

> If the manager were here, Madam, he would attend to you at once.

4.44 The subjunctive is also found in certain formal noun clauses following on a main verb that requests or suggests something:

> I propose that this topic *be* ruled out of order;
>
> The Company has ruled that no one *enter* without a pass.

It can be seen, in the first example, that *be* carries a meaning of *should be*. In the second sentence *no one enter* means that no one *may* enter.

4.45 If the subjunctive is the mood of thought or uncertainty, the indicative must be the mood of fact or certainty. Do not confuse the subjunctive *if*-clauses with *if*-clauses in the indicative mood which speak of facts or actions balanced against each other.

> If a man has sold beer on a Sunday morning, it is no defence that he has saved the life of a fellow-creature at the risk of his own. If he has harnessed a Newfoundland dog to his little child's carriage, it is no defence that he was wounded at Waterloo.
>
> Macaulay: Essay on Lord Clive

Transition
4.46 A **transitive verb** is one that must have an object to

complete its meaning; the verb passes or carries over the action from the subject to the object:

The cook *beats* the eggs.

Beats is transitive because it must happen to someone or some thing. On the other hand, we have two **intransitive verbs** in:

The patient *sneezed* and *flinched.*

One cannot *flinch* anything so it is a verb that never takes an object. Even if the patient were to *sneeze twice*, it remains intransitive because *twice* is an adverb and not the object. It is, in fairy stories, possible to sneeze gold or frogs, but in more serious work, it is hardly worth the effort of assaulting the nature of a wholly intransitive verb. There are fewer intransitive verbs than transitive ones, but there are many that act in both ways. Unfortunately the fact that many verbs have two functions sometimes leads people to treat them cavalierly.

> The youth had been before the court on two other occasions and no doubt the magistrates felt that this time they should restrain.

The magistrates were not, as the sentence stands, proposing to *do* anything *to* anybody and the reader is left with the sense of something missing or an impression that the youth was about to be passed through a colander for the second time. *Restrain* must have an object, even in court. Any doubts about the transitive nature of a verb can be resolved by using the dictionary. The letters i. and t. after a verb indicate to which group it belongs.

4.47 The transitive nature of verbs is linked with the relationship of the subject to the action. Is the subject the prime mover of the action or its recipient? In discussing transition, we must also consider **voice.**

Voice
4.48 The subject of a sentence can be hero or victim of

action: doer or done-by. A statement can be changed without altering its basic meaning by reversing the subject and object if, at the same time the verb is changed from the active to the passive voice or vice versa.

The monkey kicked the jack-rabbit.

That statement is in the **active** voice. If we were to change the position of the nouns it becomes

The jack-rabbit kicked the monkey.

This gives us two quite different statements. They seem to describe the progress of a fight because the actions shown are not the same. If, however, we wish to show that the monkey was the aggressor and that the jack-rabbit did not fight back we can reshape the first sentence as

The jack-rabbit *was kicked* by the monkey.

which is an unlikely story but has the same sense because it is in the **passive** voice.

4.49   The passive voice can be used to give a measure of formality, even authority, to a statement.

The Board has asked me to present the Report

has less weight than

I have been asked by the Board to present the Report

because the subject is no longer *the Board*, but *I*.

4.50   A transitive verb can become intransitive when it is put into the passive voice.

The Queen *banished Raleigh* on discovering his marriage to Bess Throckmorton.

This can turn to

> After the Queen discovered his marriage to Bess Throck-
> morton, *Raleigh was banished.*

Auxiliary Verbs

4.51 The verb is not only the word on which the meaning
of the sentence pivots. It is also the absolute determinant of
time. If we read that

> yesterday we will go to the Acropolis,

we instinctively discount the adverb, *yesterday*, as an obvious
error because the verb, by means of its auxiliary, *will*, tells
us that the action has not yet taken place.

4.52 Auxiliary verbs are added to the principle parts to fix
the period of any action or state. Of the thirteen tenses
shown in **4.34**, only two, the simple present and the simple
past, are without auxiliary help. The most important auxiliaries are *to be* and *to have*. The other major auxiliaries are
shall – will, should – would, may – might and *can – could*.
We also make use of verbs like *do – did* and, in some constructions, parts of obsolete or little-used verbs like *must,
ought, dare* and *used*. Many of these verbs can act as notional
verbs, with full meaning in their own right. In

> I have my cat for company

to have is a notional verb. But it is an auxiliary in

> I have worked here for forty years.

4.53 In addition to their role in tense formation, auxiliaries
give idiomatic shades or degrees of meaning to statements.
An idiom is a pattern of words with a particular meaning that
has become fixed over a long period of time. The absolute
meaning is immediately recognized while the meaning of the
separate words is ignored. If a man says *I would rather not
do it*, he shows reluctance, telling you that he is against performing the action. If, however, he says *I should prefer not
to do it*, he leaves open the possibility of persuasion. The

misuse of idioms in written work, through carelessness or ignorance, can alter the whole effect of a statement.

Shall and Will as auxiliaries
4.54 *Shall* and *will*, with *should* and *would*, have lots of booby-traps for the unwary. In simple future statements the usage is straightforward. *Shall* is used for the first person; second and third persons take *will*.

I shall sing next week;

You will sing next week.

If the subject consists of the first person and another, either second or third, person, *will* is used.

You and I will sing next week.

The same sequence is followed when *should* and *would* are used, both in simple future statements and those of Future-in-the-past. But there are subtle distinctions in both *shall-will* and *should-would* which cannot be ignored.

4.55 This list relates them to their specific meanings.

1. Command or necessity in the third person:

It has been decided that he *shall* attend the inquiry.

In this instance, *shall* means *must*; he has no choice and is *compelled* to attend.

2. Force of will or determination in the first person:

No matter what you say, *I will* go.

Here *will* means that *my mind is made up*; I am determined on a course of action. To sense the difference, compare these statements:

A. I shall drown; no one will save me;
B. I will drown; no one shall save me.*

Statement A carries a sense of despair, but statement B expresses a firm intention of drowning and a refusal of help. So the formula for a simple statement which avoids the overtones just mentioned can be seen in the familiar request to a bank manager:

I should be grateful if *you would* send me a statement.

3. Obligation or duty in the third person:

He should visit his mother.

Should is the equivalent of *ought to* in that sort of statement.

4. Uncertainty in the first person:

I *would* go if I thought it worth while.;

Contrast this with the use of *should* in 2 above. There is now a sense of *perhaps; would*, used in that sense, is always followed by a qualifying clause giving the reason for uncertainty.

5. Indefinite time in the first, second and third persons:

Any meeting that *shall* take place. . . ;

Whatever decision *I shall* take. . . ;

6. Desire, purpose or wish in *that* clauses:

The judge intends that the sentence *shall* be carried out.

---

*Help anyone in Scotland, however, who shouts 'I will be drowned'; it is probable that he or she will want to be saved.

I am anxious that he *shall* enjoy his visit.

It is his wish that you *should* attend.

Since *shall–will* and *should–would* carry such fine distinctions of meaning, and because they are so often confused and misapplied, they are now listed again according to *person*:

1. First person singular and plural:

   A. they take *shall* and *should* in simple future, conditional and Future-in-the-past statements:

   We *shall* make sure it does not happen again.
   I *should* like to visit Rome.
   We *should* have reached Bangkok on Monday.

   B. they take *will* in statements expressing obstinacy or determination:

   I *will* arise and go now . . .
   We *will* get the contract, come what may.

   C. they take *would* in indefinite future statements expressing wishes, desires, conditional intentions or possibilities:

   I *would* accept if I were asked.
   We *would* travel to Kuala Lumpur under those circumstances.

   D. they take *should* in statements expressing duty or obligation:

   I *should* telephone the Clerk of the Court about the verdict.
   We *should* visit our parents this weekend.

   E. they take *shall* in expressions of doubt or questions:

   I wonder whether we *shall* get there in time.

2. Second and third persons, singular and plural:

A. they take *will* and *would* in simple future, conditional and Future-in-the-past statements:

They *will* make sure that it arrives safely.
He *would* like to visit Rome.
You *would* have reached Bangkok on Monday.

B. they take *will* and *would* in statements expressing determination or obstinacy:

They *will* take matters into their own hands.
He *will* tease the cat even when told not to.
You *would* go to the meeting although you had been warned.
Single she *would* stay and marry she *would* not.

C. they take *would* in indefinite future statements expressing wishes, desires, conditional intentions or possibilities:

If asked, he *would* accept.
They *would* have been very bad judges of an accusation brought against Jenkinson or against Wilkes.
Macaulay: *Essay on Warren Hastings*

D. they take *should* in statements expressing duty or obligation:

He *should* investigate the matter.
They *should* behave in a more professional way.

E. they take *shall* when the speaker is making a promise, prognosticating or threatening:

You *shall* hear from my solicitor.
East is East and West is West, and never the twain *shall* meet.
Kipling: *The Ballad of East and West.*
And he *shall* be unto thee a restorer of thy life.
Ruth IV. 15

F. they take *will* in expressions of doubt:

Surely he *will* not agree to it.

G. they take *shall* in questions:

Shall you allow her to go to the Regatta?

The usage of 1.B and 2.E is illustrated by a familiar quotation from the Bible.

> For whither thou goest, *I will* go; and where thou lodgest, *I will* lodge; and thy people *shall* be my people and thy God my God.
>
> Ruth I. 16

And the following quotation illustrates 2.G and 2.B.

> And *shall* Trelawney die?
> Here's twenty thousand Cornish men
> *Will* know the reason why.

May and Might. Can and Could

4.56 The uses of *may, might, can* and *could* seem, at first glance, to hold few stumbling blocks. Perhaps their apparent simplicity explains why they are misused so astonishingly often. Although *might* is technically the past tense of *may*, both words are used as auxiliaries in the present and future tenses. They are in no way negative, but lack a positive quality. Compare

I may go abroad next year

with

I might go abroad next year.

Wilfred Whitten (John O'London) explains the difference: the first expresses a half-intention, the second a half-doubt. If you are uncertain about the reception of your suggestion you ask

> Might I propose?

but you are only being polite when you ask

> May I propose?

4.57 In written communications, *may* and *might* are used formally, therefore, to indicate polite diffidence, with degrees of certainty,

> May I take it that . . .
> You may like to consider . . .

or uncertainty

> You might like to consider . . .
> Might we assume . . .

4.58 If someone says

> You might expect that . . .

you know that he does not think that you have yet formed such an idea. If, on the other hand, he says

> You may expect that . . .

it can mean either that it is possible that you have such an expectation, or that you are being warned of a possible occurrence. In the past tense there is an even finer shade of meaning.

> You might have expected that . . .

tells you that, had things been otherwise, your expectation would have been well-founded. However, in

> You may have expected that . . .

the speaker is indicating that you were mistakenly hopeful.

4.59 Most mistakes occur in the **optative mood.**

> We hope it may not come to . . .

The optative is a mood expressing wish or desire and refers, therefore, to things which have not yet happened. The sentence above desires that things shall not turn out badly; it is not authoritative or positive, like

We hope it will not come to . . .

In

It might be better if we met to discuss it.

we have an indication of choice and a fairly firm assertion, saying that the meeting ought to take place. In the optative mood, when you are only hoping that the meeting will take place, there must be a change of tense in the verb following *may*:

It may be better if we meet to discuss it.

In this mood, *may* and *might* have dissimilar overtones in expressing permission or invitation.

I hear you plan to visit Bogota. You might visit the musum when you arrive.

Might visit has the effect of a polite invitation to do so. If the writer had said

You may visit the museum when you arrive,

permission would have been granted in a rather authoritarian way. If you write to someone suggesting that they *might* have lunch with you, there would probably be a pleasant reaction. If, however, you suggest that they *may* have lunch with you, they will resent your condenscension and nip off smartly in a huff.

4.60 Children learn the distinction between *may* and *can* at mealtimes.

Can I have the last piece of cake?

Yes, you *may*.

Can implies competence, ability or validity.

He can run very well.
The baby can crawl now.
There can be no objection.

The future is expressed by *could* in some constructions.

There could be no objection.

Could also carries a sense of possibility. Notice the different meanings conveyed by these very similar sets of opening words:

It could be advantageous . . .
It should be advantageous . . .
It would be advantageous . . .
It will be advantageous . . .
It may be advantageous . . .
It might be advantageous . . .

It also means possible achievement, rather than certain achievement.

He could win easily

gives an implication of condition. We infer that there is an *if*-clause to follow. Again, there might be a qualifying clause, beginning with *or, because* or *since*, telling us why he might or might not win.

4.61 Before we leave this group of auxiliaries, consider these examples:

I might do it, but I will not.
I may do it if I can.
I could do it but I may not.

The first implies that the matter has been considered and a

choice made. The second shows an attitude of indifference even if circumstances allow the action to take place. The third indicates that the speaker knows that it would be possible, but permission will not be given.

Lesser auxiliaries
4.62 If the chief characteristic of an auxiliary verb is its unbreakable connection with the principal parts of other verbs to indicate time, then the verbs we are to look at now only just qualify. Yet we use them constantly to augment other verbs. They can hardly be said to make new tense forms but they change the action described by the verb.

> I *like* to dance;
> I *go* fishing on Thursdays;
> Every week they *went* driving together;
> He *must* perform the task;
> I *do* not believe that;
> I *need* to see the map;
> He *used* to take a nap in the afternoon.

Closely examined, the words *like, go, must, do, need* and *used* are combined with a **gerund** or an **infinitive** (often the infinitive without *to*), and not with the **past** or **present participle**. Moreover, these auxiliaries will be inflected themselves, leaving the gerund or infinitive unchanged:

> I *liked* to dance;
> I *went* fishing;
> I *did* not believe that;
> I *needed* to see the map.

The past tense of the auxiliary gives the time; these auxiliaries are properly employed only in the **present** and **past simple tenses.** We cannot say

> I was liking to dance.

The construction is changed and we employ another auxiliary to move into the **past continuous** or **Future-in-the-past tenses**:

I used to like to dance.
I should have liked to dance.

4.63 Nowadays the verb *to use* has two chief meanings. The first is notional: to employ tools, objects, etc., to avail one-self of something. The second is auxiliary: to be accustomed to something, to do something habitually. Both these meanings must carry forward to the thing employed or the custom enjoyed; it is a transitive verb, requiring an object. The first meaning must be followed by a noun; the second is followed by an infinitive. The preposition *to* directs attention to the habit. In the next two examples, the difference is apparent.

He used to take a nap in the afternoon

tells us that over a period of time in the past the subject was in the habit of sleeping after midday, but would seem not to do so now.

He used a nap in the afternoon as an excuse for not seeing visitors.

Used in this example is a notional verb. He employed an excuse or a reason. But in

He had been used to taking a nap in the afternoon,

we have a more complex statement. At some distinct moment in the past, the subject had already accustomed himself to an afternoon sleep. To achieve this, *used* is acting as a notional verb again, with the auxiliaries *had* and *been* before the gerund, *taking.*

4.64 Some words, like *must* and *ought, shall* and *should*, are never more than auxiliaries and never act as notional verbs.

He ought to return the car.

Most others can be auxiliaries or notional verbs as the occasion demands.

I hardly dare to ask

shows how fine the distinction may be. Since *dare* often functions colloquially as a notional verb,

How dare you!

it is easy to overlook the full meaning of the statement:

How do you *dare to speak* or *to behave* like that.

Dare is a feeble word, needing its association with another verb. *Will* and *need*, on the other hand, can stand up for themselves:

I willed myself to finish the course;
I need food.

4.65   Auxiliary verbs, then, fall into distinct groups. Some have the fundamental duty of tense formation, like *to be* and *to have*. Others assist in tense formation while imparting precise degrees of meaning. Still more play an occasional part as auxiliaries. Many have another existence as notional verbs. The writer needs to be certain of the role he or she wishes them to perform in a statement and of the meaning attached to that role, in the special circumstances of person and sense.

It is natural that obligation *should* be felt, and if I *could* feel gratitude, I *would* now thank you.
            Jane Austen: *Pride and Prejudice*

Chapter Five
Building bridges

Bridges between Words – Prepositions

5.1 The Shorter Oxford English Dictionary defines a preposition as a word that relates two notional words: nouns or pronouns and verbs that are not used as auxiliaries. The second word is usually a substantive: a noun or pronoun. This does not make prepositions much clearer than the usual explanation which says that a preposition precedes the noun or pronoun that it 'governs' to show the relationship of time, place, case and so on. Definitions are all very well, but they are only useful when they put into words something at least partially understood. One needs to know just what a preposition does for nouns and pronouns. Equally, one needs to get into the habit of examining verbs used in writing and their prepositional relationship to following substantives.

5.2 For the Roman reader there were five cases that had to be recognized; Latin, as an inflected language, had the nominative, accusative, genitive, dative and ablative cases. We know some of these today. The nominative and accusative cases represent the subject and object respectively. The genitive case is that of possession and in English we indicate ownership by placing the preposition *of* before the word. The dative case was the case of the indirect object and, in English, is preceded by *to* or *for*. The preposition is often omitted and we understand the case that is meant because the construction is idiomatic.

> She gave me a book; (*to* me)
> Henry brought James a toy engine; (*for* James)
> He did me a favour. (*for* me)

The ablative case is one of agency or instrument and, in translation from the Latin, uses the prepositions *by*, *with* or *from* before the word.

> Samson slew a thousand men *with* the jawbone of an ass;

The melon was crushed *by* a tank;
The acrobat was fired *from* a gun.

There is a distinction between *by* and *with*. If *by* is the equivalent of *by means of*, the meaning of *with* is much closer to *using*.

5.3   Obviously the important part played by prepositions in saying exactly what we mean is due to case: the circumstances surrounding a word in a sentence. Since, however, there is a wide variety of statements to be made, and situations to be described, in written and spoken language, even in Latin there are prepositions to increase the scope of expressions. There is a difference between

He is from Newcastle

and

He has been away from Newcastle for years.

There is also a difference between

He is a statesman of distinction

and

Fred is the son of Henry.

In the first sentence, *of distinction*, can be turned into an adjective: *He is a distinguished statesman*. In the second sentence, *of Henry* is in the genitive or possessive case and the statement could be written as

Fred is Henry's son.

5.4   So the preposition (1) can show the case of a word in a sentence; (2) can form a phrase equivalent to an adjective: *a town in Shropshire* becomes *a Shropshire town*; (3) can form an adverbial phrase: *He treated it with contempt* becomes *He treated it contemptuously*; or (4) it can indicate position, direction, time, manner and other circumstances. We also have to discriminate between the idiomatic use of the infinitive after certain verbs and nouns and the preposition *to* when it has a special meaning: *in the direction of, as far as, in comparison with* and so on. The idiomatic use of the infinitive will be found in Appendix II.

5.5 There is little point in taking up space to list prepositions. There are few words used as prepositions which do not also function as other parts of speech. Instead, it is more practical to learn to recognize prepositions by the use to which they are put. Here, for example, are some of the prepositional uses of the word *by*, listed according to the relationship shown:

> Place or Position: He stood *by my side*;
> Agency: I was stopped *by the police*;
> Time: *By night* or *by day*;
> Manner: *By the pricking of my thumbs*;
> Instrument or Agent: She was hit *by a brick*;
> Measure or Extent: He is gaining *by inches*;
> Belief: I swear *by my life*.

And the same sort of listing can be shown for *to*:

> Direction: I took a taxi *to the bank*;
> Destination: All roads lead *to Rome*;
> Reference: It is not drawn *to scale*;
> Comparison: They were outnumbered two *to one*;
> Inclusion: We must add more rum *to it*;
> Infinitive of purpose: I wish *to remind* you ... ;
> Infinitive of result: He only does it *to annoy*... ;
> Indirect object: Lend your trousers *to John*.

5.6 *Knowing one when you see one*: Because so many words function both as prepositions and as adverbs, remember that a preposition *governs*, and is always associated with, a noun or pronoun. A word that does not have a substantive to govern, or receive the action, is a different part of speech.

Across is a preposition in

> *Across* the wires the electric message came . . .

but in

> He walked *across*.

it is an adverb modifying *walked*. In

> He drank *down* his wine/He drank it *down*.

down is an adverb modifying *drank*. But in

> He ran *down* the hill.

down is a preposition governing *the hill*. Here are some examples of prepositions used as adverbs.

Put *on* your gloves.	Put them *on*.
Take *off* your coat.	Take it *off*.
Lift *up* your hat.	Lift it *up*.
Push the pile *over*.	Push it *over*.
She gave *in* her report.	She gave it *in*.
The sun went *in*.	
The plane took *off*.	
Pull the rope *through/round/along/over*.	
Run *along* now.	

5.7 *Myths, misconceptions and misuse*: It is sometimes believed that *between* must only refer to two things; if there are more than two, *among* must be used. Pay no attention to this fallacious notion. *Between* can be used to express a simple relationship:

> She pressed the flower *between two* pages.

or we can use its wider meaning (blessed by the Oxford English Dictionary) to relate something to 'many surrounding things severally and individually'.

Agreement was reached *between the members of the Board.*

Among is less particular. It carries a sense of vague, unspecified relationship with a collection of things or persons.

He saw Miss Purdy *among the hundreds* dancing wildly;
A pebble *among others* on the beach.

5.8 If you feel that you must use *with a view to*, take care not to slip the preposition from its leash and find yourself *with a view of*. The first phrase is ugly; the second, if put in the same context, is just nonsense. A view *of* something is what a window or a lookout has. When *from* is used to denote the passage of time, it must be teamed with *to*:

She is staying with me *from* Monday *to* Wednesday.

Verbs that have a connection with the same activity do not necessarily take the same preposition:

He was *charged with* stealing a donkey.
He was *involved in* stealing a donkey.

The peculiar and particular preferences of some words for particular prepositions will be found in Appendix II.

5.9 *Bombast and bunkum:* Fear of appearing unimpressive or unimportant leads to the use of pompous prepositional phrases:

> with reference to;
> in relation to;
> in regard to;
> in the case of;

when, in most cases, they are quite unnecessary. Too often they are squeezed into the context like a superfluous shirt pushed into a holiday suitcase. Some are so frequently used that they have become vulgarisms. Readers know just what sort of low-level letter they have received when they spot one of these pieces of hokum:

Until such time as . . .
In respect of . . .
As to whether . . .
As to why
As in the case of
So far as . . . is concerned . . .

5.10   Avoid, where you can, the use of present participles as prepositions. They are often the first step on the road to gobbledygook. *Considering everything. . . , regarding the. . .* or, even worse, *respecting the* . . . may, on occasion, pass muster as spoken constructions. In written work, especially formal letters, they are uncouth, encountered in the most backward of Government departments; moreover, they can easily lead one into the trap of the 'dangling' or unattached participle (**4.23**). Sometimes there is no alternative to *with regard to* . . . or *with respect to*, but most of the time they can be discarded in favour of ordinary conjunctions or prepositions.

5.11   *The road I was coming out of*: Some popular books on grammar are still perpetuating the Victorian precept: do not end a sentence with a preposition. While pointing out that it is no longer a Dreadful Crime, they still regard it as a solecism, and something to be avoided. Nineteenth-century grammarians had to go a long way back to find their dubious authority for the interdict: the word *preposition* is derived from the Latin *praepositio*, which means 'to put before'. The strict application of the rules of Latin grammar to modern English is, because of the historical development of the language, nonsensical. The fashion probably began when Dryden, who died in 1700, took a sudden dislike to the end preposition. Great men are allowed their eccentricities but we do not all have to go round chopping down trees for fun just because Gladstone found it a pleasant relaxation. Place the preposition before the substantive or use it as the final word as sense and harmony dictate.

Bridges between Thoughts – Conjunctions
5.12   A conjunction conjoins; it forms a connecting link

between words, clauses or sentences. The most obvious and ubiquitous one is *and*. To see why we need and use conjunctions, we have to look at the principal unit of expression: the sentence. The words in a sentence are put together to make a sentence – that is, to say something about a thing, a person, an event or a feeling. Very simple statements give little trouble,

> Roses are red

and

> Jack went up the hill.

If, however, we know that Jack was not alone, wending his way up the hill, and that

> Jill went up the hill,

we can use a conjunction to combine the two statements as

> Jack and Jill went up the hill.

5.13 Conjunctions are divided into two groups, according to the function they perform: **co-ordinating** and **subordinating**. They are further divided according to the part they play in adding to the meaning of a statement: **conjunctive** and **disjunctive**. Many, like prepositions, have already appeared as other parts of speech and now pop up as conjunctions, like a history teacher who takes a woodwork class in the afternoons, does a milk-round first thing in the morning and has a part-time job as a croupier in a gambling club.

5.14 Sometimes two separate statements, each capable of standing independently, are joined, or co-ordinated, by a conjunction.

> My dog has gone *and* I am desolate.

More often, extra, or subordinate, pieces of information have to be tacked on to the central statement, making dependent clauses.

> Jacky shall have but a penny a day *because he can't work any faster.*

The co-ordinating conjunctions
5.15   Co-ordinating conjunctions link words

>   ham *and* red cabbage,

and clauses

>   He invited me, indeed, to see his harem, *but* he made
>   both his wives bundle out before I was admitted; he
>   felt, as it seemed to me, that neither of them would bear
>   any criticism.
>   Kinglake: *Eothen*

and sentences

>   Marriage is, therefore, a lottery, *and* the less choice and
>   selection a man bestows on his ticket the better.
>   Thomas Love Peacock: *Nightmare Abbey*

The subordinating conjunctions
5.16   Noun clauses and adverbial clauses are ushered into
the sentence by subordinating conjunctions. These are the
clauses which do not form a complete statement in themselves, or which make statements that would seem irrelevant
without their connection to the main statement.

5.17   *Noun clauses*: Most **noun clauses**, when they are not
the subject of a sentence, form the object and are generally
preceded into the sentence by *that*. We have met *that* before,
as a demonstrative pronoun; and its pronoun origin explains
its use as a conjunction.

>   I know *that* my Redeemer liveth

is a more succinct and impressive way of saying

>   My Redeemer liveth; I know *that*.

Noun clauses after *that* often occur after verbs that express
abstract feeling:

fear, hope, imagine, feel, doubt, believe, etc;

verbs that express a direct or positive statement:

> announce, say, admit, agree, remark, teach, demand, recommend, stipulate, threaten, promise, command, warn, propose, reveal, demonstrate, declare, etc.;

verbs of desire or expectation:

> expect, hope, estimate, presume, assume, wish, suggest, etc.;

verbs of perception:

> see, observe, notice, perceive, hear, think, discover, realize, recognize, etc.

You will notice that what you say, hear, see or feel or notice is always expressed by a noun clause.

5.18 Of course the verbs in that list can occur in other constructions, some of which will be found in Appendix II. Noun clauses can also be introduced by other words acting as conjunctions.

> He understands *how* the machine is constructed.
> They threaten *to* dissolve the Company.
> *Where* she lives is a secret.

5.19 *Adverb clauses*: **Adverb clauses** are groups of words that contain a finite verb (**4.12**) and play the part of an adverb in the sentence. If we look again at

> Jacky shall have but a penny a day, because he can't work any faster,

and examine the ideas it contains, we can see that

> Jacky will be paid one penny a day; fast workers get more; Jacky cannot work fast.

The clause *because he can't work any faster* is doing the work of an adverb of cause or reason. The conjunction that introduces an adverb clause tells us what adverbial function it is carrying out. We can list these conjunctions accordingly:

Adverb Clause of	Conjunction
Place:	where, whither, whence;
Reason or Cause:	because, since, for, as;
Time:	when, before, after, while, since, till, until, as;
Purpose:	so that, in order to, in order that, lest;
Condition:	if, unless, in case;
Manner:	as if, as, as though;
Comparison:	as, than;
Concession:	although, though, even if.

and here are examples of each one:

Place: This is the house *where* I live;
Reason: He ran away *because* he was frightened;
Time: She had to leave the ball *before* the clock struck twelve;
Purpose: They buy flour in ten-pound bags *so that* it will last;
Condition: I refuse to go anywhere *unless* you go too;
Manner: The frog hops down the path *as if* the stones were hot;
Comparison: She was *as* beautiful as a butterfly;
Concession: I give to charity *although* I have little to spare.

5.20 It is obvious that the conjunction does more than just glue parts of a sentence together; it is essential to the meaning of what you are trying to say. Using the wrong conjunction (and many people do) can create unnecessary ambiguity and may give an impression of ignorance. Be sure that you have considered the implications that lie in any conjunction you use. Here is a list of the general purport of some of the most commonly-used conjunctions:

> *although:* notwithstanding, in spite of the fact that;
> *after:* in the time after that at which. . . ;
> *and:* together with;
> *as:* inasmuch as*, because, since;
> *because:* so that, for the reason that, in order that;
> *before:* in the time prior to;
> *but:* except, on the contrary, without;
> *for:* seeing that, since;
> *if:* in the event that;
> *since:* seeing that, inasmuch as*;
> *though:* in spite of the fact that;
> *till:* up to the time that, until the point when;
> *until:* as *till*;
> *while:* during the time that, simultaneously, although, at
> the same time.

For the full meaning of any conjunction you propose to use, see the dictionary recommended in Appendix I.

5.21 *Adjective clauses:* An adjective is a well-behaved word; it knows its place, which is usually before the noun it qualifies:

> a charming song; a knotty problem.

It does not have to stay in that place to be understood. We know just what is meant when we read the description,

> a simple cottage, snug and warm,

and when someone says,

> the bed is comfortable.

We take these in as *a simple, snug, warm cottage* and *a comfortable bed.* In every case there is a noun, the antecedent which is qualified by the adjective: *cottage, bed* or whatever substantive is referred to. The **adjective clause** behaves like an adjective; to do so, it is introduced by a relative pronoun, or a word acting as a relative pronoun, which harks back to the necessary antecedent. In other words the adjective clause

---

*Use only when there is no alternative. It can give a pedantic impression.

must have something to describe and must be preceded by a word that tells us which thing in the main statement is being described. Where agreement is concerned, there is an important distinction. The word introducing the clause agrees in person, number and, if necessary, gender with the antecedent, but its *case* is determined by its own subjective or objective role in the *clause*.

> The architect, who designed rather strange houses, sat at the end of the table,

but

> Lady Moggery, about whom there was a good deal of gossip, put her elbow into the finger-bowl.

To see what often goes wrong, look at this sentence:

> Frederick, whom they said was dead, arrived suddenly at eight o'clock.

In the first sentence, *who* is the subject of the clause – *designed rather strange houses; whom,* in the second sentence, is the object of the clause *there was a good deal of gossip about....* The third sentence contains a horrid mistake: the relative pronoun introducing the clause should be in the nominative case because it is the subject of the clause. It is corrected to

> Frederick, who, they said, was dead, arrived suddenly at eight o'clock.

If you are uncertain about the case in which a relative word should be, try turning the clause into an independent sentence and substituting a personal pronoun for the relative word.

> *He* designed rather strange houses;
> There was a good deal of gossip about *her*;
> They said *he* was dead.

5.22 *Correlative conjunctions*: These conjunctions hunt in pairs and you will get nowhere if you try to use one on its own. The exception is *whether; whether*'s partner, *or not*, is always implied in the construction even when it is not seen.* Those most often encountered, and often abused, are:

> not only . . . but also
> both . . . and
> as . . . as
> such . . . as
> so . . . that
> either . . . or
> neither . . . nor.

The last two are victims of careless confusion. *Or* can only partner *either* and can never mate with *neither*. But it is quite common to read sentences like

> She has neither talent or ability.

If the poor thing has no gifts, we should say that

> she has neither talent nor ability.

In the sentence

> It was such a moon as this men saw before the great storm.

you cannot say *such a moon which men saw. Not only – but also* and *both – and* suffer from misplacement. In

> A messenger was not only sent, but also a man from the office went round. The door was never answered.

the meaning has been turned upside-down and the emphasis has vanished. *Not only a messenger was sent but also a man from the office* is still awkward but intelligible. The original awkwardness arose from the desire to use as much emphasis as possible in spite of the fact that the second statement was

---

*Example: I do not know whether he will agree to it (or not).

incompatible. The sentence is much better without the correlative conjunctions;

> A messenger was sent and a man from the office also went round. The door was never answered.

Sometimes people feel that they must use *either* when offering alternatives.

> When assembling the ingredients either make sure everything is chilled or things taken from the refrigerator can be used.

The result is obviously wrong; *make sure everything is chilled* does not match *things taken from the refrigerator can be used.* The writer has not realized that the same parts of speech or type of phrase or clause must follow each half of a pair of correlating words. If the first word precedes an adjective or a noun, the second must also precede an adjective or noun.

> The kinkajou climbs by using *both strong claws and a prehensile tail.*

The phrase or clause that follows each half must also match.

> When assembling the ingredients, *either make sure* that everything is chilled, *or use* things taken from the refrigerator.

Each one of the pair of correlatives is now followed by a verb and the tenses of the verbs agree.

5.23 A common mistake is to use part of a compound conjunction when the two words together have a special meaning.

> In handling seedlings, hold them by the leaves. Do not pull them up by their stems *else* you will damage them irreparably.

It is wrong to use *else* when you really mean *or else.* In that sentence it would have been better to use *because.*

5.24 *Clauses of comparison*: In everyday use, the conjunctions that help to describe things or to compare them to one another are usually straightforward:

> This cauliflower weighs *as* much *as* that one,

and

> . . . *as if* this earth in thick fast pants were breathing. . .

are simple constructions. However the continuing, though shadowy, presence of case in English can be shown by the pronouns used after *as*. If the accusative or objective case follows, it produces one meaning:

> I love you as much as *him*,

which means that the love mentioned is divided equally between the person addressed and some other fellow – *as I love him*. If *as* is followed by the nominative, or subjective, case,

> I love you as much as *he*,

the implied verb *does*, after *he*, tells us that the person addressed is loved by both the speaker and some other fellow to the same degree.

5.25 The tenses used with correlatives must relate to the same period of time, in most cases:

> Either he is right or I am,

not

> Either he is right or I was.

But when one thing is compared to another, the time of the objects compared need not be the same. We can compare the past to the present;

> As you were, so I am now,

and the past to the future:

As I was, so you will be.

5.26 *Conjunctive and disjunctive conjunctions*: The conjunctive conjunctions are those which guide the two parts of the sentence towards the same end: *as, because, for* and so on. Disjunctive ones introduce a statement in opposition or an alternative: *but, though, or,* etc. Don't stray into the error of using them as written 'ers' and 'ums'; if a conjunction does not enlarge the meaning it has no business to be in the sentence. It is annoying for the reader to scrabble about looking for an alternative or a contrary statement, only to find that the conjunction just slipped in while the writer paused for thought.

It was impossible for me to reach London to receive the award, though, so I could not attend.

Though, in that sentence, is entirely superfluous: *though* what? Doubling-up, or using two words that convey the same meaning in the same sentence, is known as tautology. Don't say *limited only to; only* is unnecessary when you say *limited to.*

He pulled, unavailingly, at the knob, but could not open the door.

Use *unavailingly*, or but, not both. If it availed him nothing to pull at the knob, he couldn't open the door, could he?

He pulled at the knob but he could not open the door.

Bridges for Readers – Sentences
5.27 The cultivation of a feeling for language and the development of discrimination depend on the writer's determination to express a precise meaning in what he or she puts on paper. Since English no longer relies on an inflection to indicate the subject (or primer of the verb) in the shape of the verb itself, and cannot fall back on case-endings to show

the parts played by different words in sentences, other conventions must be employed. The structure of sentences must carry all the information that was once given by changing the form of words.

5.28 A sentence is a group of words expressing a thought. That thought may be concrete or abstract; it can be a direct statement from the speaker, or a statement about a person or thing; it must always, whatever form it takes, be complete. The subject is the point of origin of the sentence. Except in the imperative mood, the subject is named and represented by a substantive; that noun or pronoun will be related to the verb in person and number. The identification of the subject is reinforced by the order in which words are put together: sentence structure.

5.29 In most sentences, the subject is recognized because it precedes the verb.

A director disrupted the meeting.

In such simple sentences, the noun, noun phrase or verbal phrase that follows the verb is the object. As we often compose sentences that contain more than a subject or a verb, the part of the sentence which makes a statement relative to the subject – predicates about the subject – is described as the predicate.

Logicians think clearly.

The words *think clearly* are a predication about *logicians*. (The sentence is to be regarded as merely an example, not an unassailable truth.) Be quite clear about the meaning of predication. It has nothing to do with fortune-telling or prophecy (prediction); it is an assertion. The predicate makes an assertion about the subject.

The floodwaters *inundated all low-lying areas.*

5.30 While this word order is significant, it is not absolute. We transpose words to frame a question:

Is he ill?

and expand meaning and scope by putting adjectives, adverbs, phrases and clauses into the basic structure. Although we make changes in the shape of the sentence, they are never random alterations. In English sentence structure always relates to meaning.

5.31 Analysis is the process of breaking down a sentence into its component phrases and clauses, picking out the principal clause and relating the other parts to it. **Parsing** is the examination of each word in a sentence, identifying the part of speech to which it belongs and examining its relationship to other words in the sentence. It is very useful to be able to do this. An understanding of the relations between parts of the sentence and between the words in a sentence underlies the acquisition of a sensitive ear for mistakes and a firm command of written language. Unfortunately, the dissection of sentences from the repertory of classic poetry and prose often created as much loathing for the work dissected as for the process itself. The melancholy charm of Crashaw's epitaph for a young couple who died and were buried together,

> To these, whom Death again did wed,
> This grave's their second Marriage-bed.
> For though the hand of fate could force
> 'Twixt Soul and Body a Divorce,
> It could not sunder man and Wife,
> 'Cause they Both lived but one life,

vanishes under the grammatical knife. But you should, at least, be able to investigate your own unsatisfactory work and put it right.

5.32 Look at a literal translation, intended to show English children how a German sentence should be constructed:

> Mama! In the milkpail a dead mouse is.
> Oh! Have you it thereout getaken?
> No, but I have therein the cat gethrown.

It is a useful exercise in the simplest sort of analysis. To give the sentence an English form we take the subject, *a dead mouse*, first, putting the verb next, followed by the adverbial phrase, *in the milkpail*.

A dead mouse is in the milkpail.

This, however, suggests a degree of deliberation. The mouse, for reasons of its own, chose to expire in the milk. But the speaker is concerned because there is a foreign object in the pail which should hold only milk. Using an introductory word and changing the order, Mama is informed that something is wrong:

There is a dead mouse in the milkpail.

Here the Latin convention of using the verb *to be* as an equals sign comes into effect; one can see, for example, a similarity between *There is* and the French *Il y a*. The mouse is still the subject although it follows the verb.

5.33   The next two sentences, in their English form, move further from the German. Not only are the compound adverbs *therein* and *thereout* discarded, as *in* and *out* serve the purpose very nicely, but the prefix to the verb, relating to time, has also been lost. Yet the sequence of events is perfectly clear:

Have you taken it out?
No, but I have thrown the cat in.

5.34   The first statement tells of a situation that exists at the time of speaking: the pail contains a dead mouse. The second and third sentences deal with matters that have occurred before the child spoke to its mother. Mama wants to know what has been done and finds out, too late, that, as a result of action already taken, the pail now holds the cat as well as the mouse.

Components of the Sentence
5.35   The main sentence (or main clause) is a complete

statement to which other components of the sentence relate. Adjectives and adverbs increase the scope of words; phrases and clauses increase the scope of the sentence. From a simple assertion, it becomes one that is particular and more definite as the added components describe the subject or object and indicate time, place, purpose and other factors.

5.36 *Phrases*: A phrase is a group of words, with no finite verb, which has a bearing on part of the main clause.

> Adverb phrase: Everyone was fascinated *by her charm*;
> Gerund phrase: Have you considered *travelling by train*?
> Participle phrase: *Alarmed by the noise*, I got up.

5.37 *Clauses*: A clause is a group of words that has a finite verb and may be a subordinate statement, depending on the main clause.

> Adverb clause: I walk *whenever the weather is good*;
> Adjective clause: He is the man *who tweaked the parson's nose*;
> Noun clause: I realize *that I was mistaken*.

5.38 *Sentence types*: The simple sentence needs no intro-duction. The **compound sentence** has to contain at least two co-ordinate clauses. They need not be of the same weight or importance but each must be a complete assertion in its own right, and they are joined by a conjunction or a word acting as a conjunction. The **complex sentence** has at least one dependent clause, subordinated to the main clause. Complex sentences offer more chances for mistakes.

Examining the Works

5.39 The watchmaker knows how to take the ailing clock to pieces in order to find the fault. If something seems to be wrong with a sentence, it must be taken apart to track down the mistake. The simplest way is, first, to separate the phrases and clauses; then, to number them. Practise on a healthy sentence.

> 'Come in, whoever you are! Don't mind the dogs!' shouted little Mr Bouncer, as he lay, in an extremely

inelegant attitude, in a red morocco chair, which was considerably the worse for wear, chiefly on account of the ill-usage it had to put up with, in being made to represent its owner's antagonist, whenever Mr Bouncer thought fit to practise his fencing.

Start with the main clause.

1. . . . shouted Mr Bouncer

which, for the sake of convenience, we will turn round.

1. Mr Bouncer shouted . . .

What Mr Bouncer shouted is the object of the main clause, and consists of two statements in the imperative mood, the first of which has an adjective clause introduced by a relative pronoun, *whoever*. More important, for our purposes, are the other phrases and clauses which make up the bulk of the assertion.

2. as he lay;
3. in an extremely inelegant attitude;
4. in a red morocco chair;
5. which was considerably the worse for wear;
6. chiefly on account of the ill-usage it had to put up with;
7. in being made to represent its owner's antagonist;
8. whenever Mr Bouncer thought fit to practise his fencing.

5.40 In investigating the way in which the component parts fit together, use a much-simplified form of analysis. Classify the phrases and clauses in two ways; according to their grammatical function: noun, adjective or adverb; and according to their roles in the sentence: co-ordinate, subordinate or dependent. Look, also, at the contribution they make to the meaning of the whole sentence.

Clauses
5.41 *Adjective clauses*: These clauses describe either the

subject or another noun in the sentence.

> 5. a (which-was-considerably-the-worse-for-wear) red morocco chair:

Adverb clauses: These, like adverbs, establish place, manner, time, reason, etc., and generally act as adverbs.

> When (Time) 2. as he lay;
> Why (Reason) 6. on account of the ill-usage it had to put up with;
> Why (Result) 6a. (that) it had to put up with;
> When (Time) 8. whenever Mr Bouncer thought fit to practise his fencing.

Phrases
5.42 *Adverb phrases*: These behave in an adverbial way, as do the clauses, but they have no finite verb.

> How (Manner) 3. in an extremely inelegant position;
> Where (Place) 4. in a red morocco chair.

Gerund phrase: 7. in being made to represent its owner's antagonist.

5.43 When the parts of the sentence are put back together again, describe the action of each part as it affects other words, or parts, of the whole statement.

> 1. is the main clause, consisting of the subject, *Mr Bouncer*, and a predicate: *shouted 'Come in, whoever you are! Don't mind the dogs!'*;
> 2. is a subordinate adverb clause of time, modifying *shouted* and telling when Mr Bouncer shouted;
> 3. is a subordinate adverb phrase of manner, modifying *lay* and telling us how Mr Bouncer lay;
> 4. is an adverb phrase of place, modifying *lay* and telling us where Mr Bouncer was when he shouted;
> 5. is a subordinate adjective clause, introduced by the relative pronoun *which*, qualifying *chair*;

6. is a subordinate adverb clause of reason or cause, modifying the verb *was* in 5. To clarify the relationship, and find the subject and verb, rephrase the clauses: It (the chair) was worn *because* it was ill-used;

6a. is a subordinate adverb clause of result qualifying *ill-usage*;

7. is a gerund phrase referring to *it*; it is the object of the verb *had to put up with.* Rephrase 6. and 7: It (the chair) had to put up with being made to represent its owner's antagonist;

8. is subordinate adverb clause of time, introduced by the conjunction *whenever*, telling us when the chair was ill-used.

5.44 The purpose of this disentanglement is to check the relationship between all the parts of the sentence. At the same time, it is possible to look at the cases of pronouns and the tenses (and their sequence) of verbs. Not only must the person and number of verbs match their subjects, but a verb in a clause which relates to the subject of the main clause must match also. Main and co-ordinate clauses have to be complete sentences; it must be possible to trace the basic assertions, even when interpolated phrases and clauses separate subjects or objects from their verbs. The sentence used as an example was taken from *The Adventures of Mr Verdant Green*, by Cuthbert Bede, otherwise Edward Bradley, (Blackwood: 1853). It would be a useful exercise to find other complex sentences to analyse yourself and to discover, in the same way, a compound sentence.

5.45 Undertake the parsing of a sentence only when a problem seems intractable. Simple analysis should find most faults, which can then be corrected within the phrase or clause in which they occur. But occasionally word-by-word examination can't be avoided. Use Chapters Three and Four to discover your mistakes; tracking down errors yourself and learning your weaknesses is a more valuable way of learning than reading examples of parsing.

Ellipsis

5.46   In both spoken and written English we use **ellipsis**, a word derived from Greek words, meaning 'come short'. It is the omission of words that would complete the sentence in the ordinary way. In particular, it refers to the leaving out of words that will make no difference to the reader's understanding. The sense is there even if the words are not; the meaning is implied. If, for example you are asked to do something, and you answer

> No,

you are really saying

> No (I will not do it).

The use of ellipsis can produce a pleasantly casual style, almost conversational in tone.

> Not the most exciting companions, they were still valued friends.

If we insert appropriate words (in parentheses), to take the place of those that are missing, this can be arranged as either a compound sentence

> (they were) not the most exciting companions, (but) they were still valued friends,

or a complex sentence with a dependent clause

> (Although they were) not the most exciting companions, they were still valued friends.

5.47   The hazards encountered in the use of ellipsis show up when writers leave out more words than the sentence can spare with safety.

> The Chairman was forced to resign and the managers dismissed.

There is a singular subject, *chairman*, which has a singular auxiliary verb. Unfortunately the *managers*, plural, are trying to swing on the singular verb which will not bear their weight.

> The Chairman was forced to resign and the managers were dismissed.

5.48 Sometimes *that* is omitted, to shorten a sentence or avoid repetition. But *that* is essential after any part of the verb *to be* and its absence, in other circumstances, can make an inelegant and incorrect sentence.

> Mr Smith asserted Mr Dodd was wrong and should not have acted without authority.

The oversight in that statement concerns the verb *assert*. You assert *something* about somebody. The co-ordinate clause looks forlorn without a clear subject.

> Mr Smith asserted that Mr Dodd was wrong and that he should not have acted without authority.

It is worth reminding yourself that the verb you use must be able to support everything that depends on it, and that leaving out the antecedent for a pronoun can make a subject meaningless. If you are going to omit a relative pronoun, make sure that its invisible presence will still be felt by the reader. Opportunities for fudging sense lie at the tip of every pen.

Confused voices
5.49 If you forget whether you have made your subject the hero or the victim of the action, you can fall into error. It confuses the reader, too, if you begin a sentence in one voice and end in another. Watch out for the 'impure' passive construction; prefer *I hope* or *we hope* to *it is to be hoped*, for example. 'Impure' passives are those which follow an active verb in this sort of construction.

> The sentence that is intended to be written;
> The alterations that are proposed to be made;
> The question it is anticipated will be answered.

The correct equivalents are

> The sentence you intend to write;
> The proposed alterations;
> The question to be answered.

5.50 People working in Civil Service Departments and in large companies tend to adopt a passive impersonality, as if they themselves had nothing to do with the contents of their letters or texts; it all arrives by Divine inspiration.

> Your application has been noted and . . .
> It has been decided that . . .

Where has the subject gone?
5.51 Use of the passive voice can trap the writer into forgetting that the subject of the sentence has changed.

> The cats' piteous mewing were heard.

If it had been spoken, the speaker would have noticed the mistake at once. It *feels* wrong. Concentration was on the *cats* and a decision to use a passive verb probably came too late. The subject is, of course, not *cats*, but the noise they are making – mewing, which is singular. The sentence could be reformed as

> The cats' piteous mewing was heard

or

> The cats were heard mewing piteously.

Agreement
5.52 Verbs and their subject must agree, like riders on a tandem bicycle. Some constructions are apt to upset the partnership and agreement is lost. if a sentence is to have meaning, the subject must be identified beyond doubt. In

> The man kicked his dog,

the subject stands out as the brute who mistreats his friend. *Kicked his dog* is an equally identifiable predicate. There is only one dog-kicker involved, so the subject is singular; the verb is in the third person and the past tense. The unfortunate *dog* is the object. This is simple stuff; but composing a sentence like

> As one of those who was directly involved, I declare an interest,

is not quite so straightforward. The main clause, *I declare an interest,* rightly has a singular verb, but the subject of the adjective clause is not *one*; it is *those,* and needs a plural verb.

> As one of those who were directly involved, I declare an interest.

5.53 These inclusive subjects sometimes lead writers to be overcareful about antecedents.

> All of us remembered his teaching and its effect on them.

All may sound impersonal, but *us* defines the group as one of people at least known to each other and probably present at the time of speaking. *All of us* is the qualified antecedent and requires a pronoun in the first person plural as the indirect object:

> All of us remembered his teaching and its effect on us.

If the statement had been

> All of those he taught, myself included, remembered his teaching and its effect on them,

those would have been the antecedent and the third person pronoun would be correct.

Losing the way
5.54 When a road is being repaired and you are diverted through a number of side streets you can, in the confusion, miss the turning back to the main road. A complex sentence, with clauses inserted between the subject and the main verb, offers the writer opportunities for losing direction and using the wrong verb form.

> The difficulty facing the economy, including the inflation rate, which has been expected to rise, and massive public expenditure, are analysed in the document.

The inflation rate, rising or falling, and public expenditure are added ornaments. *Difficulty* is the subject. It is still singular and wants a singular verb:

> . . . is analysed in the document.

If, however, you look at the sentence closely you will see that the real error lay in the singular subject, which ought to have been *difficulties.*

> The difficulties facing the economy, including the inflation rate, which has been expected to rise, and massive public expenditure, are analysed in the document.

The Spoken Word on paper
5.55 *Oratio recta* and *oratio obliqua* are the sonorous terms used to report what people say. The first, 'straight speech', is a way of writing down the words just as they were uttered by the speaker.

> 'Indeed' said Jefferson, 'I tremble for my country when I reflect that God is just.'

Oratio obliqua, or 'bent speech', is more likely to be useful to the writer of texts, reports and essays. It requires a number of changes, the first of which is to abolish the quotation marks. The writer is now reporting hearsay; the sentence must move from the present to the past tense. The first person can't be used because the writer is a bystander; the pronoun must be in the third person.

> Jefferson said that he trembled for his country when he reflected that God is just.

Notice that, although the other verbs have moved into the past tense, the verb in the last clause has been left in the present, because the judgement of God is an immutable truth. (4.36)

Another Road Through the Wood

5.56 For one reason or another, it is often necessary to rewrite. It does not follow that the statements you have already made, if they were accurate, must be altered. The shape can be changed without losing any of the meaning. Reworking the construction of a sentence is probably all that you have to do. English offers, perhaps more than any other language, a choice of forms in which statements can be made. This flexibility is very useful in varying the presentation of ideas and in giving a sense of personal style to your work.

> Though the King stood alone, with nobles estranged from him and the Church against him, his strength seemed utterly unbroken.
> R.H. Green: *History of the English People*

This could be rephrased as

> The King's strength seemed utterly unbroken, although he stood alone, with nobles estranged from him and the Church against him,

or as

> Though the nobles were estranged from him and the Church was against him, so that he stood alone, the King's strength seemed utterly unbroken.

Packaging

5.57 At times we need to put a considerable amount of information into a short or limited space. If the ideas and presentation are well organized, this can be done without any loss of sense or meaning.

> A four-foot tall robot (or unidentified walking object, UWO) spent the night in Beverly Hills police station after it was spotted walking along exclusive Beverly Drive, lights flashing from its skull.

This sentence, with a shorter one, 'Its remote-control operator did not come forward', was an entry in a column for brief news items in *The Times*. The writer had to include all the interesting information he could in a small space. The robot's description is given by two adjectives (four-foot tall), a parenthetic insertion (or unidentified walking object, UWO), and an adverbial clause (lights flashing from its skull). We also know what happened to it (spent the night in Beverly Hills police station). Moreover, we know how it came to be arrested (spotted walking) and where (Beverly Drive). Even the nature of the area where it rambled is given (exclusive). It is a good example of facts packed succinctly.

5.58 Sentence building, then, if it is to be well done, involves paying attention to grammar – the specific relationships and meaning of words – and to syntax – the technique of using words grammatically in a sentence.

In addition to using the conventions for things like reported speech properly, the writer must be able to take a troublesome sentence apart in order to diagnose mistakes. It is a skill which comes with practice.

Chapter Six
Making the text live

Punctuation

6.1   When we speak, either conversationally or addressing an audience, we modulate our sentences, using stress, pauses and vocal inflection to make meaning clear. In speaking, we drop our voices during part of our sentences, or stress one word to show emphasis. The last word is sometimes slightly pitched up. We include or exclude clauses from the main part of a sentence by using both a lower pitch and inserting parenthetic pauses, like invisible brackets. To deny emphasis to less important parts of what we are saying we will use an even tone and a somewhat faster rhythm. We also grimace, raise our eyebrows, frown and smile.

6.2   Take all the stops out of a passage of three or four lines – or better still, get someone else to do it for you. Then read it aloud. You will find that you have to have several goes to sort out the separate sentences and will have to re-read it again to decide where emphasis should fall. Clauses that should be set off from the main sentence becomes confusingly entangled. If there is a group of words qualifying a noun, and some are nouns in their own right, it will be hard to decipher the meaning of the group.

6.3   Reading is a complex skill, learnt consciously but, once mastered, practised without conscious thought, like driving. As driving is undertaken with the intention of reaching a destination, so reading is done for the purpose of extracting meaning. A journey to a place unknown would be more difficult if there were no signs and no white lines. The road does not tell the driver where he or she is going.

6.4   A page of music shows a sequence of notes; but, musically speaking, a mere sequence of notes is not a composition. Written music, therefore, has a system of symbols, a code, that enables the composer to show the key and the rhythm in which the piece is to be played; to indicate the length of individual notes and the stresses on them; and to measure the duration of intervals and pauses.

6.5   Punctuation is the notation system for written English. It is not just an ornament; it is meant to convey to the reader's eye exactly what you want to say by modulating it as if you were speaking. Properly used, it indicates what is important in a statement, where emphasis is placed, and what is secondary to the main assertion.

Full Stops
6.6   There should never be any difficulty about the full stop. It is there to mark the end of the sentence. However, the stream-of-consciousness school of fiction popularized the idea of using disjointed phrases or clauses beginning with capital letters and ending with full stops. Band-wagon jumpers followed suit in less appropriate circumstances. If I take some liberties with a passage from James Bryce, the effect will be obvious:

> In very early times the tribe chose a war chief. Who was, even if he belonged to the most noble family, no more than the first among his peers. With a power circumscribed by the will of his subjects.

This should be all one sentence. By placing stops after *chief* and *peers*, I have made the reader work harder, rootling about for relationships. *Who* begins a **relative clause** describing *chief* and should be set off with commas. Rootle as he may, the reader will find no subject for *with* in the last sentence because it is not a sentence but a dependent clause attributing something to *chief*. To make amends to James Bryce, let me show the sentence with its original punctuation.

> In very early times, the tribe chose a war chief, who was, even if he belonged to the most noble family, no more than the first among his peers, with a power circumscribed by the will of his subjects.
>> James Bryce: *The Holy Roman Empire*

Lesser stops

6.7 It is often harder to decide where to use colons and semi-colons. If one thinks of stops as nails, the full stop is a 3-inch nail, driven home firmly; the colon is a 1-inch wire nail and the semi-colon is a panel pin.

The colon

6.8 Use this stop to introduce a list of things:

apples, soap powder, coffee, toothpaste and cheese;

or ideas:

Epicureanism, Platonism, the Peripatetic School and Monism;

or people:

Edmund Burke, Lord Clive, Warren Hastings and Sir Elijah Impey.

If you are reporting a long verbatim statement use it after the name of the speaker.

Captain Winterbottom: I should inform you that Lieutenant Murgatroyd was standing beside the aircraft when I saw him. He took a small bugle from his pocket. When he had blown it, he began to eat the port wing.
Judge-Advocate-General: Did he put anything on it first?
Captain Winterbottom: No, sir. The use of salt, sauce or any other corrosive substance is contrary to Queen's Regulations.

6.9 Do not use a colon followed by a dash (:-). It serves no purpose, is old-fashioned and makes a text look cluttered. It is worth abandoning the habit, if you are one of the addicts, and saving yourself a small amount of unnecessary typing.

The semi-colon
6.10 Semi-colons have more uses. They have more weight than commas, but are less divisive than colons. Where a sentence contains antithetic clauses, it is appropriate to separate them with a semi-colon. They are then still obviously related to each other but their opposition is made plain.

> In India he had a bad hand; but he was master of the game and he won every stake. In England he held excellent cards, if he had known how to play them; and it was chiefly by his own errors that he was brought to the edge of ruin.
>
> Macaulay: *Warren Hastings*

6.11 It can also be used to divide two sentences, either of which might stand alone but which need to be closely related. This is very much the case when they are too long to be separated by a comma.

> Insult passed into open violence when the Bishops' Courts were invaded and broken up by Protestant mobs; and law and public opinion were outraged at once when priests who favoured the new doctrines began openly to bring home wives to their vicarages.
>
> J.R. Green: *History of the English People*

My personal inclination would be to remove the superfluous *and* after the semi-colon in that sentence as a matter of style, though not of rule. Conjunctions are seldom needed after semi-colons, but there are times when it can improve the sense to use one.

The comma
6.12 The most troublesome stop, for most people, is the comma. A fellow-student at my university was a brilliant biologist but could not punctuate. After writing an essay or report, she would look over it and sprinkle a few commas in at random, like parsley on soup. When taxed with this, she explained that the text looked naked without them; as she did not know their function, she used them as ornaments.

6.13 Commas are pauses which set apart a word or clause. For this reason they must never separate a subject or object from the verb unless they are used on either side of an interpolated word or clause.

> My black cat, who died at the age of fifteen, had a crumpled ear.

The *cat had a crumpled ear* is the main sentence. The clause *who died at the age of fifteen* is neatly set off from the sentence by its two commas. If, on the other hand, I had put the comma after *had*,

> My black cat, who died at the age of fifteen had, a crumpled ear.

the meaning of the statement would be obscured. In the last paragraph there is an adverbial clause, *when taxed with this*, giving the time of the explanation, so I set it off with a comma before beginning the main part of the sentence. *As she did not know their function* is another adverbial clause, and it, too, gets a comma.

6.14 This setting-off is even more important when the clause is placed between two parts of the sentence, as in the *black cat* example. When the sentence is part of an academic text, this setting-off is essential.

> Such a spirit was, before the last century or two, wholly foreign to art as well as to metaphysics.

The more complicated the statement, the more commas are needed. The following passage is an intolerably unwieldy sentence by today's standards. However, it is a good example of the modulating effect of commas. Read it aloud, pausing slightly at each comma and see how the sense becomes clear in spite of the length.

> And thus, when we remember that the notion of progress and development, and of change as the necessary condition thereof, was unwelcome or unknown in

mediaeval times, we may better understand, though we do not cease to wonder, how men, never doubting that the political system of antiquity had descended to them, modified indeed, yet in substance the same, should have believed that the Frank, the Saxon, and the Swabian ruled all Europe by a right which seems to us not less fantastic than that fabled charter whereby Alexander the Great bequeathed his empire to the Slavic race for the love of Roxolana.

James Bryce: *The Holy Roman Empire*

6.15 There is also a particular use for commas where several qualifying words are used with one noun. Where the qualifiers are related to the noun, all but the adjective closest to the noun are separated by commas.

She was a gorgeous, bouncing, cuddly armful.

Sometimes the one closest to the noun is a sort of interpolation or afterthought. In that case the comma rightly comes just before the noun.

It was my very own, never-to-be-forgotten, day.

Commas are never used between adjectives that qualify each other.

He had a dark grey saloon car.

6.16 Commas create confusion when they are badly placed. I have described punctuation as a notation system. In music the sequence of notes tells the performer *what* is to be played; *how* it is to be played is shown by the notation system: the shape and appendages of each note, the time and key signatures, and the bars. Punctuation is the indication of *how* a thing is to be read. If the marks are in the wrong place or omitted, writers will fail to get messages through because meanings are uncertain.

His instructions were supposed to be adequate by some, though not the majority of his hard-working students.

Some may include people not attending his classes, but it is clear that most of the hard-working students think his instructions inadequate. If we put a comma after majority, there is a complete change of meaning.

> His instructions were supposed to be adequate by some, though not the majority, of his hard-working students.

Judgement is now confined to the group of hard-working students, some of whom are quite happy with his instructions.

6.17 Here is an example of a meaningless placing of commas, taken from 'junk mail' that came through my letterbox.

> We are pleased to make available to you, an opportunity that could prove very profitable. It's a chance for you, within this limited period to increase your financial security by participating in a program of financial planning.

It is possible that this writer believes that there should always be a comma after the word *you*. It is more likely that the comma in the first sentence is there through carelessness. The comma after *you* in the second sentence makes one dash to the end of the sentence to see what will happen after the *limited period to increase your financial security*. Because there is no comma after *period*, the reader can assume that you must prove your worth by investing elsewhere before availing yourself of the *opportunity*.

The hyphen
6.18 Those indispensable marks, hyphens, have been through a period of decline, when many editors felt that they were old-fashioned and put readers off by frightening them. The fact that the popularity of the parenthetic dash (**6.24–5**) rose at the same time may have had something to do with their distaste for the hyphen. Copy-editors went through manuscripts, religiously removing all the hyphens, regardless of the effect that this would have on meaning. Some, falling more heavily into the mire, left hyphens which should have been removed.

6.19 As hyphens are among the marks most needed to make meaning clear, it is worth identifying the circumstances which call for them.

1. There are the ambiguous or dual-purpose words which must be recognized by the reader for what they are. A hyphen after the prefix distinguishes the verbs that tell of repeated actions and other compound verbs from those that are spelt in the same way but have a different definition. Most of these words begin with the prefix *re*.

re-laying the carpet	relaying the message
a re-covered sofa	he has recovered
an in-patient	in patient submission
re-pair breeding stock	repair the damage
re-counted votes	a recounted tale
a re-enforced rule	re-inforced concrete
play is a re-creation	children enjoy recreation
re-sign here	he must resign

As well as differentiating one meaning from another, hyphens are used to get rid of awkward letter-combinations that might confuse, like re-elect, re-edit, re-enter, re-enact, re-establish, pre-empt and pre-ignite. Generally, following mathematical usage, *co-ordinate* is used without a hyphen and many people recognize *cooperation* and *cooperative*. You should decide whether your readers' ability to sort the word out will allow you to omit them; I have a preference for the hyphen in co-ordinate. Do not, however, leave the hyphen out of *co-opt*. In all these cases the hyphen changes the point of stress, as in *restrain* and *re-strain*. Always use a hyphen after the prefix if the following word is based on a proper noun and starts with a capital letter.

2. In the English of England certain prefixes are hyphenated: *anti-*, *pre* and *non-*. Hyphens are used with these prefixes when they would otherwise produce an unfamiliar word: *anti-anarchy*, rather than *antianarchy*, *pre-decease* is preferred to *predecease, preperceptive* should be *pre-perceptive* and *non-usage* is better than *nonusage*. In the

States there has been a tendency to remove the hyphens from words of this sort; you can see the result above. My advice would be to use the hyphen wherever it improves comprehensibility.

3. A term that ordinarily consists of two words, like Court Martial or Executive Committée, remains as two words when it is the nominative (subjective) or accusative (objective) case. The moment it has to be put into the possessive, it needs a hyphen: the Court-Martial's findings; the Executive-Committee's decision. It is also hyphenated when used as an adjective.

> The meeting had a sombrely oppressive, Court-Martial, atmosphere.

Under 3 we should include words formed from constructions that imply possession or contain the word *of*: the *eye of the bull* becomes the *bull's eye*, the editor of copy is the *copy-editor* and the list of words is a *word-list*. As a reminder of the way in which hyphens are used to make a compound possessive when you cannot think of a more graceful way of expressing ownership jointly held, I offer this quotation:

> She drank prussic acid without any water
> And died like a Duke-and-a-Duchess's daughter.
> R.H. Barham: *The Tragedy*

4. The hyphen is most active in sorting out descriptive words when several are applied to one noun. If some of the qualifying words are nouns in their own right, it can be hard to discriminate between the adjectives and the qualified words.

> A cheap record player

is one which apparently plays cheap records, until a hyphen makes it a cheap *record-player*.

> The Long Haired Cat Club Show

leaves one to wonder how *long* the *show* is, and whether bald cats are excluded. It needs a hyphen between *Long* and *Haired*. In

a heavy craft workshop

and

a home management area

the reader must lose a moment in deciding which is heavier, the *craft* or the *workshop*, and in working out whether the management *area* was in the *home*. Corrected, the statements are obvious.

a heavy-craft workshop
a home-management area.

Where technical descriptions are involved, hyphens are vitally important.

self propelled underwater missile homing equipment

needs three hyphens to make sure that the reader picks up the details at a glance:

self-propelled-underwater-missile homing equipment.

When the words used could easily have a second meaning. it is well to be careful to make the one you want quite clear.

the lost wax process;
the slave driver,

are confusing. Are we sure that the process isn't lost? Is the driver a slave? Perhaps I mean

the lost-wax process;
the slave-driver.

5. The misplaced hyphen is just as bad as the absent hyphen. Fowler quotes an advertisement for

a superfluous hair-remover

which obviously nobody wants. Similarly, a

skin rash-relief

must be something laid over the skin. The importance of marrying the word that qualifies is shown in this example:

Anti-child labour laws have been passed.

What a frightening prospect! No doubt the legislature were looking for suitable salt-mines.

6. There are clear distinctions in meaning between some compound words that can be joined together, take a hyphen or appear as two words. You can buy a *secondhand* watch; see that its *second-hand* is moving; and be pleased that it has a *second hand*. We blackball someone wanting to join a club by dropping a black-ball, which is a black ball used to register a negative vote, into a container.

The general tendency is for compounds to lose their hyphens and become one word as they come into general use, and are easily recognized as single words: *hodcarrier, homecoming, manhandle*. Among new arrivals are *countdown* and *splashdown, nearby* (this must not be confused with *near by*), *goodbye, watercolour* and *fallout*. Beware of those words that usually appear with hyphens but cannot be combined. Many of these have another meaning when they are unhyphenated:

a turning-point	a turning point
a put-up job	he puts up with it
a bull's-eye	a bull's eye

Hyphens are never used when the predicate is qualified or modified:

a well-known man	is well known
a common-sense idea	makes common sense

a good-will gift	is given with good will
an ill-served meal	is ill served
up-to-date news	is up to date

Dashes and Parentheses

6.20 Before looking at the use of these marks it is as well to understand that the printer regards ( ) as *parentheses*. Brackets are the [square] enclosing marks used to enclose comments, notes or translations added by writers or editors to work by another hand.

6.21 Parentheses are used for interpolations: the stray thoughts or 'asides' put into a main sentence. They are never preceded by a comma – what would be the point of adding another stop? – but are sometimes followed by one in cases where a comma would have fallen if you had not added the extra two-penn'orth. You cannot put parenthetic material into quotes inside the marks – again, it would be a useless exercise; but you can put quotation marks about any word in the phrase which would have deserved them without the parentheses. How confusing this seems: examples would be better.

It was Lady Hainault (the long Burton girl, as Madam Adelaide called her) come home from her last party.

If you want to, you may do this:

(the 'long' Burton girl, as Madam Adelaide called her)

but you may not do this:

('the long Burton girl, as Madame Adelaide called her').

6.22 A whole sentence can be put into parentheses.

He began striking spitefully at where he thought the dog was, with his stick. (The dog was evidently used to this amusement and dextrously avoided the blows.) Finding vertical blows of no avail, the blind man tried horizontal ones, and caught an old gentleman across the shins, making him drop his umbrella and catch up his leg.

6.23   Anything in parentheses is a break in direct narration or exposition. It follows that writers should use them sparingly; the reader is chiefly interested in your keeping to the point. Plunging straight into writing on the typewriter can lead the most organized writers to have little extra thoughts after they have embarked on a sentence. They are then tempted to use a dash and stuff in the brilliant new thought. There is nothing wrong with the parenthetic dash if it is used properly and in moderation. Strictly speaking, if the dashes are equivalent to the parenthetic marks, they should open and close, just as the marks do. However, G.V. Carey (*Mind the Stop* – see Appendix I) suggests that a dash can be used as a single mark, if what it encloses is at the end of the sentence. As he says, dashes do not have to perform in pairs. If the enclosure is completed *before* the end of the sentence, you must close it with a second dash.

6.24   I have noticed that some writers use a dash when they depart from the original or basic construction of a sentence, and then fail to go back and finish the sentence. We get the first half of the statement and then, like John Jones's Kit-cat-astrophe, it gets the whole Atlantic for its waist and is 'doomed to break off in the middle'. It exasperates the reader. Check for sense and continuity when you edit your work.

Exclamation Marks

6.25   The exclamation mark is a printed version of the bugged-eyes-raised-eyebrows expression. It really must be used with self-restraint. Properly, its place is after exclamations or brief imperative statements:

> Heavens!
> Go home!

If there is a genuinely surprising remark to be made, an exclamation mark shows that you expect the reader to be astonished. It ought to put you on your mettle to make sure that he is. Don't, whatever you do, put exclamation marks in parentheses; it looks like a vulgar sneer.

Question Marks
6.26 There are few apparent pitfalls in using question marks. Do they go at the end of questions? Of course they do. However, you must avoid using them in reporting speech indirectly.

> They asked why had they not been told?

You are making a statement about what they asked, not asking a question of your own, so it must be shorn of the mark and given a full stop.

> They asked why they had not been told.

If you put question marks in parentheses at any time, it will appear that you question your own veracity or accuracy.

Quotation Marks
6.27 Typewriters are equipped with two sorts of quotation marks: single and double. I don't think I have ever seen a manuscript in which the author has used these marks in accordance with the accepted form for printed work. If a single word is quoted, use single quotations marks.

> the 'iron' Duke.

6.28 If you are including quotations of differing lengths, only those of less than five lines are given quotation marks. These are *always* single marks. The only time that double marks are used in non-fiction texts is when there is a quoted word or sentence within a quotation. The practice is to work inwards from single to double marks.

6.29 Quotations that are longer than five lines are 'displayed'; that is, they are indented to set them off from the text. Don't use a lot of short quotations. It breaks up the appearance of the page. The text will look better if you vary them by treating some as indirect quotations. Never forget that if you use any part of another author's work, you must clear copyright, except when you use a brief indirect quotation.

> Ellacott said that if a squall blew up, the upper sails had to be taken in while the ship was still under way.

The Apostrophe
6.30 In **3.46** the use of apostrophes in possessives was discussed. Since it was thoroughly examined, I will only remind you that apostrophes are never used in the possessive form of *it*, but they are used to abbreviate *It is* to *It's*: It's a fine night. There is also special usage in proper names ending in *s*, and this is also covered in the same paragraph.

Vocabulary – The Raw Material
6.31 No one can tell you what words to use when you write. The fact that critics are longing to tell you that you have used the wrong word should not cause you any anxiety. I say 'should not' because you will, of course, have made yourself familiar with any word, and its generally-accepted meaning, before you set it down. A word that is not fully understood should never appear in any written work.

6.32 Words are the stuff of communication. The writer needs to have the widest possible vocabulary from which he or she can pick and choose what best suits the work in hand. We are not born with a large bagful of words in which we can rummage at will. Words must be sought and learnt. I am not suggesting that every day you should ingest five new words from the dictionary like vitamin pills. The dictionary is the checklist, not the source.

6.33 In your reading you will come across unfamiliar words. Stop and look them up; then go back and look at them in the context in which you found them, a practice which will give you an even better understanding than the dictionary definitions. Don't search out abstruse words and work them into your text like lardoons in a joint of veal. The result is always self-consciously priggish and can raise a laugh that you would rather not hear.

6.34 'New' words, in this sense, are those you have not encountered before. They may also be those of whose application you have been uncertain. Writers who read widely have an advantage, for they can find words to cull from other writers. Nevertheless gathering other men's flowers must be done with circumspection. Words that are too far from ordinary understanding are of little use. Impressive words are not measured by length but rather by the precision with which they match the sense of what is said.

Stumbling blocks

6.35 Precision depends on the right word being in the right place at the right time. The wrong word causes a break in the communication between writer and reader. The right word with the right meaning may have been in your mind, but you have mis-spelt it. On the other hand you may, in haste, have picked out a word that seems close to your meaning but which has overtones that may create an impression far from your intention. There are some words that regularly give trouble. Some have the same sound but are not spelled in the same way and have different meanings according to the way in which they are spelt: the **homophones**. Some are words that have closely related meanings and are often substituted for each other: the **synonyms**.

6.36 *Homophones*: Homophones have no problems for the speaker, whose hearers are guided by the sound and the context. Moreover, if they have doubts, they can ask the speaker to clarify them. But if you do not spell well naturally, the word on the page may bear no relation to the word in your mind, and the reader may puzzle over it or write you off as an ignoramus. Some are very familiar words and mistakes are due to carelessness. If you have spelling problems you should learn them by heart:

to–too–two; their–there; in–inn; ring–wring;
right–rite–write; sight–site.

6.37 Words less often used cause trouble because their meanings have something in common, but their usage is particular to the circumstances in which they are found.

a. DRAUGHT (noun and adj.): you .have a *draught* horse; drink a *draught* of ale; buy *draught* beer; feel a *draught* of air; play a game of *draughts*; haul in a *draught* of fish; see the *draught* of a ship and watch a *draughtsman* draw.

b. DRAFT (noun and verb): you *draft* a speech; get a banker's *draft*; and see a *draft* of *drafted* soldiers.

a. PRACTISE (verb): you *practise* your craft or profession; *practise* your game of golf; and you can be a *practising* chiropractor.

b. PRACTICE (noun): you take up the *practice* of practising what you preach; *practice* makes you perfect; your doctor may be in a group *practice*.

a. DEPENDANT (noun): you support your *dependants*.

b. DEPENDENT (adj.): your dependants are *dependent* on you.

a. STATIONARY (adj.): the train is *stationary* in the station.

b. STATIONERY (noun): you buy *stationery* from a stationer; you have office or personal *stationery*.

a. GAUGE (noun and verb): you travel on a narrow-*gauge* railway; a rain-*gauge* measures rainfall; the standard measure of things from barrels to bullets is their *gauge*; you *gauge* the distance or the precise measure of something.

b. GAGE (noun and verb): you deposit a *gage* as security;

you throw down a *gage* to challenge an opponent; you *gage* yourself to fulfil your promise.

a. PRINCIPAL (adj. and noun): the first use of *principal* is as an adjective meaning *chief* or *most important*: the *principal* reason for education is preparation for the future. It is used as a noun to describe *a chief functionary in certain circumstances*; he is the *principal* of the college.

b. PRINCIPLE (noun): This describes a fundamental truth (moral *principles*) or a general law of science or nature: Werner's *Principle*: the earth is a child of time.

6.38 *Synonyms*: The similarity of sense (or closely related meaning) of synonyms is both a convenience and a nuisance when one writes. Very few words mean exactly the same thing, so that a hasty snatch at any word that will do because you can't remember a better one at the time may alter the message to the reader. The whole point of writing even the simplest communication is to hit the nail of meaning on the head. Does your chosen word have the exact sense that you have in mind? Can *pride* and *arrogance* substitute for one another? What is the difference between *distinct* and *distinctive*? Are you *sympathetic* or do you *pity* someone? What if the word, though temptingly close, is not really synonymous? Here are some words that are not synonyms but are often mistakenly made to stand in for each other:

a. CONTINUOUS: something that is continuous is unbroken, without interruptions: a *continuous* thread; a *continuous* process; a *continuous* mountain chain.

b. CONTINUAL: a continual occurrence may recur at intervals but goes on, on and off, for a long period: the *continual* howling of the neighbours' baby.

a. EXERCISE: to train oneself; to use a faculty or power; to discharge a function; to stretch one's abilities or intellect: *exercise* your wits; *exercise* your right to vote.

b. EXERT: a stronger word than *exercise*, it means to bring to bear a force or quality; to strive *to do* something; to strive *for* something: he *exerted* his influence.

a. EFFICACY: this means *having the desired effect* and is applied only to things, usually medicines.

b. EFFICIENCY: applies to persons and, to a lesser extent, to machines, *Efficacy* is never used of personal agents; anybody or anything can be *efficient*, but a human being can't be *efficacious.*

a. CERTITUDE: is a *feeling* of *certainty* or conviction: I say it with *certitude.*

b. CERTAINTY: a *certainty* is *that which is certain*; a fact or truth: the existence of the Yeti is not a *certainty.*

a. DENOTE: to denote something is to mark it out, to distinguish something, perhaps a mark or sign; to indicate or be indicated by something: Sun Dialls, by the shadow of a stile or gnomen, *denoting* the hours of day; inflammation is *denoted* by the suffix *-itis*, e.g. *meningitis.* Note that *denote* has a direct association with the thing or word denoted.

b. CONNOTE: to connote is to imply or indicate something additional to the primary meaning of a word, to 'note' something with something else: justice *connotes* impartiality. A *connotation* has a secondary association with the word connoted.

a. CONNOTATION: as you can see from the word *connote*, a *connotation* means the inclusion of meanings other than the primary meaning in a word or statement.

b. CONTEXT: the text immediately around a passage or an insertion; the general setting in which meaning is determined.

a. RESTLESS: this is an adjective meaning uneasy; constantly active or wishing to be active; averse from being settled or quiet.

b. RESTIVE: *restive* is also an adjective but it means to be intractable; stubborn; unwilling or resistant to being controlled.

a. DEFINITE: positive; precise; exact in meaning.

b. DEFINITIVE: final; beyond refutation.

Selection and preference

6.39 Obviously in framing a statement one is going to choose words that convey one's meaning most exactly. Since, however, there are many different ways of saying things in English, one will select those that best fit the situation. At the beginning of the century there was a reaction against the Victorian fashion of using elaborate words and polysyllables. The Fowler brothers, in *The King's English* (Oxford, Clarendon Press: 1906) urged the good writer to prefer Anglo-Saxon words to those derived from Latin or from languages that themselves derived from Latin, and this rule is still well-regarded by many people. It is repeated in Service handbooks advising officers on the writing of reports. It would be a pity for writers to take this 'rule' too seriously; it is easy to be made self-conscious and lose the quality of natural expression. The word you should prefer is the one that best fits your meaning, whatever its derivation.

6.40 Nevertheless, the thinking behind the rule is sensible. If communication is the purpose of writing, it should be as direct and straightforward as possible. The simplest words, often the shortest, are usually best. Polysyllabic elaboration can spoil understanding and ponderous words, often used to soften harsh concepts, make ideas or plans impersonal and unreal, less likely to be taken seriously or seen for what they are. *To clean up* sounds more thorough and less frightening than *to decontaminate*; things do not have *to decompose* when they *rot*. The *next* house or room is as easy to find as the one that *adjoins*. A *global* distribution of food doesn't sound as related to the needs of the starving as a *worldwide* action would be. It is not always necessary to say *alternative*; sometimes *other* will do very well. It may be essential to your subject to put in *deoxyribonucleic acid* or *paradichlorbenzene*, but even these, after their first appearance in the text, are usually abbreviated to DNA and PDB. Above all, don't show off or use jocular terms like *logorrhea* or *osculation*. Let an *emporium* be a shop or store, unless you are prepared to let your words suffer from premature senility. Save *steatopygous* to use as a delayed implantation insult for a chair-bound opponent.

Change and decay
6.41 English, like any other healthy living language, is always growing and moving onwards. But although the language is in a constant state of flux, it is neither your business nor mine to set out to alter it deliberately. True change arises inadvertently and gains acceptance through its merits. One of the original meanings of the word *let* was *to obstruct or impede.* We can still hear the echoes of this meaning in the tennis term, *let*, which indicates that the ball was impeded in its flight, and in

> Her Britannic Majesty's Principal Secretary of State Requests and requires in the name of Her Majesty all those whom it may concern to allow the bearer to pass freely *without let or hindrance.*

This sense is now, except in tennis, archaic and *let* is always used in the sense of *allowing* or *permitting* something to happen or someone to do something. More recent change can be seen in the popular word *charisma.* This arrived, in the form *charism*, from ecclesiastical Latin, as *a God-given favour*, extended to cover a *grace* or *talent.* Hence charismatic means *talented* or *full of grace.* Popular usage has brought it to describe personality, the attribute of personal magnetism.

6.42 The change in *charisma* is innocent and useful. When a change has gained the respectability of popular currency it is pernickety and pedantic to refuse to use it. The person who refuses to eat pineapples because they do not grow naturally in England misses one of life's pleasures. Yet it is important to make a distinction between a new use and a misuse. The former enriches the vocabulary; the latter takes something from it. The vocabulary is the warehouse to which everyone who writes must go and it follows that the loss of any part of what is stored there must affect us all.

Deterioration and decadence

6.43 Advertisers tell us of the 'unique' offers that they have for us, offers which are usually repeated year after year. People speak of things as 'quite unique', as if they could be more so; even worse, 'unique' is given a false comparative – *more* unique or *most* unique. *Unique* means *positively unequalled* or unparalleled, the one-and-only-one, far too useful a word to be debased. *Superlative* means *of the highest degree*; use it to mean just that; it is a double-first of a word. Spoken extravagance is evanescent. When extravagance appears on the page it has a more concrete and lasting existence. Tell your friends that the party was *fantastic* but don't use the word to describe a play or an experiment unless you really mean it: it has overtones of eccentricity, meaning *grotesque* or *capricious*. Speaking of *grotesque*, remember that it is not an abstract term but refers to material things that can be seen or touched: a building, a sculpture or a figure on a stage.

6.44 The man who tells his friends of a *fabulous* beast may be referring to his dog or the horse that won the 3.30; but what word will he be able to use if he meets a unicorn? Or a leviathan? It is one of the characteristics of colloquial language that words, from time to time, find themselves widely and fashionably misapplied. The fashion burns itself out and another word receives popular attention. This is quite natural and in conversation the vigour of such words helps the speaker. Where the catch-word is unacceptable is in any written work, other than personal letters. If words are the currency of communication, misuse debases them and we have an increasing stock of dwindling assets.

Junk words and dishonoured phrases

6.45 Jargon finds its way into what people write far too often. Verbs are invented in fits of bravado; make-weight terms cover a poverty of thought or invention; and some words are used to show that the writer is up-to-date, like a final clutch at departing youth.

6.46 What is worst about jargon in written work is that much of the time it is mere mouthwash. Jargon originates in small groups, a sort of handy or comradely code, and spreads in closed situations: trades, professions or disciplines. Many of those who take it up don't understand it, and it drifts into meaningless ornament. It is no excuse to say that lots of people use in-phrases and popular expressions. Bad or mishandled usage can't be justified on the grounds that careless or ignorant writers find it acceptable. What's bad is bad and will remain bad. Here are two inexcusable examples of 'invented' verbs:

> The journal . . . will be *headquartered* in Europe:
> A BBC2 film season . . . *showcases* performances.

6.47 *Too big for their boots*: Puffed-up technical junkwords are self-defeating. Their presence denotes run-of-the-mill ideas which have been window-dressed with words that are expected to give the work a more original or intellectual aspect. The discerning reader will see through the disguise to the mediocrity beneath. Few people would mistake a donkey for a pretty girl because it is wearing a straw hat and a red ribbon.

6.48 It is true that dictionaries include the word *conceptualize* (they also include the words *nopal* and *glossator*, which few have been silly enough to adopt), but its popularity has increased out of all proportion to its usefulness. Many business letters, examination answers and texts are made hideous by its use and that of its illegitimate child, the noun *conceptualization*. Market research and advertising have become forcing-houses for neologisms and pseudo-technical language. *Conceptualization* is one of their worst efforts. If we go back to the original word, *concept*, we find that it means *idea* or *thought*, and is a useful alternative if not over-exposed. An *idea* or *concept* can be *imagined, produced* or *conceived.* The product of *conceiving* is a *conception.* Strike out *conceptualize* and insert *conceive* or *imagine* where you can, and never, under any circumstances, allow *conceptualization* to remain.

6.49 This may seem harsh advice to members of the discipline that uses the immutably singular abstract noun *behaviour* and a brand new plural, *behaviours* (3.8(10)). How did this misapplication come about? Perhaps it is the result of imperfect translation from another language. An educated person's vocabulary should hold a number of words for the components of *behaviour*, among them *action, reaction, manner, activity, conduct, bearing* and *demeanour.* The first four of these have both singular and plural forms; all describe material aspects of behaviour. If the misuse is irrevocable and becomes widespread, we shall have lost a valuable word without gaining one in its place. Of course, it is not the only instance. Other words are as badly misdirected and roughly handled in other fields.

6.50 Education spawns many pseudo-technicalities. For some reason people connected with the teaching profession find it difficult to call things by accepted names. The humble blackboard is a 'visual aid'; children 'receive counselling'; and teachers confuse themselves and everyone else by wallowing in terms like 'remedial class', 'pastoral care'*, 'pyramid systems', 'integrated day' and 'project work'. Unfortunately, technical gobbledygook attracts other catch-words as dust under the bed attracts slut-feathers. What should one make of the priggish term 'socially meaningful'? The opposite, 'unsocially meaningless', shows what an empty phrase it is.

6.51 Using pompous and overblown words is a sign of professional aggrandizement and indicates that you are afraid your work may not be taken seriously or, worse, that it is valueless. Professions and disciplines should take warning from 'Haigspeak'. Here is an example to match 'behaviours': at a Congressional Committee hearing, a man, asked about

---

*Nothing to do with animal husbandry — refers to children.

his possible reaction to something, answered that the question was too 'suppository',* displaying not only his pomposity, but also his ignorance.

6.52 *Overdue waste disposal*: In the 1930s hundreds of objects were produced, from chairs to table-lamps, that were described as 'modernistic'. That is to say they were fashionably crude and ugly without being functional. The fashion died out but the sturdy discards still survive in many households, refusing to wear out. The same detritus of fashion tends to persist in language, inexorably eroding precision and often driving out useful alternatives. As a copy-editor, I find texts made incomprehensible by the over-use of outworn clichés; it is my job to clarify them. Usually this means replacing a tacky word with a simpler, more direct one. A wide vocabulary may be the advantage gained from the use of a highly developed language, but it can turn into a disadvantage if it is used to muddle the reader.

6.53 Try to rephrase sentences to give a rest to these recently over-exposed terms:

> hallmark; syndrome; ambience;
> disincentive; strategic.

A *hallmark*, for example, is a more lengthy way of saying *a mark, a sign* or *a symbol*. It is probably most aptly fitted into a precept or an aphorism: Honesty in small things is the hallmark of integrity. *Syndrome* is a term borrowed from medicine; it means a concurrence or events concurring, occurring together, but it does *not* mean objects in the same place or arriving together. When the doctor or veterinary surgeon talks about a 'heart/kidney syndrome' he is misusing the word; he should not remark on the fact that all mammals expect to have both hearts and kidneys in the same body. Re-writing to by-pass these words can be a valuable exercise – especially if you take the opportunity of refreshing your knowledge of them in the dictionary.

---

*He meant hypothetical or suppositious

6.54 Have second thoughts about using any of the shop-worn terms (left-hand column); use the simpler alternatives (right-hand column) instead.

facilitate	for	ease, make easy
opt	for	choose
debilitating	for	weakening
participate	for	take part
utilize	for	use
shelve	for	put aside
adjacent	for	near, beside
prior to	for	before
numerous	for	many
ameliorate	for	improve
in excess of	for	more than
specialism	for	special subject, specialty
formulate	for	express
devolution	for	delegation
via	for	through
forwarding	for	putting forward
motivation	for	inducement, purpose
traumatic	for	shocking
amongst	for	among
whilst	for	while

6.55 Avoid using the following words:

ongoing	shakeup
grass roots	polarize
uptight	total package
benchmark	in the last analysis
individualize	personalize
organizational	at this moment in time
orientation	update
overview	force-field analysis
connectivity	problematic

Searching for bright and lively words to liven up one's subject is a futile exercise. It is possible to be enlightening, informative, pithy and even witty while using only words that are 'plain'. It is not worth going back to the past for novelty, either, as you may fall into the same trap as the man who pulled out a 16th century word and told his readers that a teacher's role was *supportive.* He succeeded in making the teacher sound like an elastic bandage when he need only have said that

>Pupils need support from a teacher

to have made his point.

The right way round:
6.56 Some words or pairs of words seem to cause confusion, either because they are closely related but have very individual tenses or uses, or because they can be mistaken for one another. Easy as confusion is, it is taken as a mark of ignorance. Each word has a particular meaning and the wrong one spoils the sense of what is said.

6.57 *An apparent overlap*: Three verbs, related but distinct from each other, cause so much trouble that it is worth identifying their peculiarities and nailing the clarification to the courthouse door. They are:

1. to lie (on the floor, beside, in the sun, etc.);
2. to lay (a carpet, a keel, an egg, etc.);
3. to lie (on oath, in your teeth, like a trooper, etc.).

The first two can be more simply referred to as *to lie (down)* and *to lay (down)*. They become confused because the present tenses of *to lie (down)* and *to lie (about something)* are the same; the past tense of *to lie (down)* is the same as the present tense of *to lay (down)*; and the past participles are very close in form: *lain, laid* and *lied*. Often it is the forms other than the present tense which tend to mix themselves up and slip into the wrong place when the unwary writer's attention is distracted. Here are the three trouble-makers:

1. *to lie (down)*:
   a. it means *to position* (oneself or itself); *to be at rest*; to *remain in position*;

b. it is intransitive, taking no direct object; it is always something done by the subject;

c. present tense: I, you - we, you, they *lie*; he, she, it *lies*;

In a cowslip's bell I lie; The book lies on the table.

past tense: I, you, he, she, it - we, you, they *lay*;

But he lay like a warrior taking his rest. . . ;

present participle: *lying*;

I am lying in the sun; The fleet is lying at anchor;

past participle: *lain*:

The last macaroon has lain on the plate for an hour.

2. *to lay (down):*
   a. it means *to place; to deposit; to impose;*
   b. it is intransitive and must have an object; it is always something done by the subject to someone or something else;
   c. present tense: I, you - we, you they *lay*; he, she, it *lays*;

   We lay the carpet today; She lays eggs for gentlemen.

   past tense: I, you, he, she, it - we, you, they *laid*;

   Slowly and sadly we laid him down.

   present participle: *laying*

   He is laying a ghost; The hen cackles when laying an egg.

   past participle: *laid*

   The law has been laid down.

Note: *lay* in *now I lay me down to sleep* belongs to this verb, not 1. I lay (or *place my self*) down to sleep.

3. *to lie:*
   a. it means to utter a falsehood; to deceive;
   b. it is intransitive, never takes an object, but can take an indirect object - I lie *to you*;
   c. present tense: I, you - we, you, they *lie*; he, she, it *lies*;

   I cannot lie with conviction; He lies about his past.

   past tense: I, you, he, she, it - we, you, they *lied*;

   When he lied, he smiled sweetly; They lied to the police.

present participle: *lying*;
   She is lying to us.
past participle: *lies*;
   I have lied and lied, and lied again.

6.58 *Lie* and *lay* have compound forms, *overlie* and *overlay*, which prove even more troublesome to people who have difficulties with the three we have just dealt with. *Overlie* means *to lie over* or *upon; to smother.* It is transitive, unlike *lie*, and has a specific geological sense.

a. present tense: One stratum *overlies* another;
   past tense: A blot *overlay* the signature;
   present participle: We sensed gloom *overlying* the meeting;
   past participle: The piglets were *overlain* by the sow.

Overlay means *to lay over* or *upon.*

a. present tense: Cook *overlays* the pastry with fruit and cream;
   past tense: calcareous algae *overlaid* the structure of the coral reef;
   present participle: the carver was *overlaying* the frame with gold leaf;
   past participle: the satin of the collar was *overlaid* with lace.

If you are ever in doubt about the one that you want, try reversing the words to *lay over* and *lie over*: fog lies over Los Angeles; the members will lay a flag over the chairman's body. Never be tempted to use the airline neologism, *layover*, to mean a break in your journey; it is based, as you can see, on an ignorant misuse of *lay*. Show your disapproval, but resist the urge to jam a foreign coin into the baggage-weighing machine next time you hear it.

6.59 Some personal pronouns give rise to doubts. When does one use *oneself* or *itself* in preference to *one's self* and *its self*? The first pronoun is used reflexively; I did it myself; the machine reverses itself. We use *one's self* or *my self* to refer to a personal identity or entity: traits of character relate to one's self. Unless you are very egocentric, you will probably seldom need to use it.

6.60 In a number of different BBC radio programmes, speakers have referred to themselves as *nauseous* because of something they have seen or heard. It is a remarkably candid self-description, as the word means *loathsome* or *disgusting*. They probably intended to say that they were *nauseated*, or *made to feel sick* by something.

6.61 Two words often seem to entangle themselves hopelessly: *imply* and *infer*; so do the nouns derived from them: *implication* and *inference*. To *imply* is to make a statement in which there is a meaning that is not expressed in so many words. *To infer* is to draw a conclusion or meaning from a statement that does not state that meaning explicitly. Mr Singh said that some persons, like his neighbours, the Jittaboys, had pets which were described as 'cats' though they seemed to resemble wild dogs. Wild dogs, as everyone knew, were savage and destructive by nature. *Imply*: Mr Singh implied that the Jittaboys' cat was savage and destructive. *Infer*: Mr Jittaboy inferred that Mr Singh was accusing the cat of being like a wild dog. *Implication*: the Jittaboys' cat had behaved savagely and destructively towards Mr Singh, and possibly towards his property. *Inference*: Mr Singh did not care for the Jittaboys' cat.

6.62 *Farther* and *further* are variations of the same word. *Farther* is still used as a comparative for *far* and in references to distance.

> Must we travel farther tonight?
> Little Boondocks is five miles farther than Great Jerkwater.

But *further* is more generally used and accepted in every instance where *farther* might occur, so it is to be preferred.

> He explored further into the jungle;
> I intend to take the matter further.

Weighing words
6.63 Look for strong and mild alternatives to suit your context. *Possess*, for example, is a positive word, strongly implying ownership. *Have*, on the other hand, covers a much wider area of meaning and is weaker. If a man *possesses* land, it is firmly in his landowner's grip, but any land he *has* can be an allotment or a small field of which he has the use. *Choice* is often made quickly or lightly; when you *select* something, there is an element of deliberation. To *mean* to do something certainly expresses an intention, but if you say that something is *intended*, the reader has a right to expect that you have committed yourself to carry it out.

Tags and abbreviations
6.64 You should only use abbreviations when it is absolutely necessary. A page peppered with *e.g.*, *i.e.* and *ms.* is not attractive and can annoy the reader if the abbreviations have been misused. *E.g.* stands for *exempli gratia* and means *for example*; write *for example* out in full and put commas before it and after the example you've used. *I.e.* does *not* have the same meaning, though many writers appear to think so; it stands for *id est (that is)* and you should always use the English words and not the abbreviation. Use the word manuscript, or typescript; it won't kill you to do so and your work will look better. Always write *per cent*. The typewriter may have a percentage sign you have been longing to use, but resist the impulse to do so unless you are sending a brief informal memo or answering an examination question. In this paragraph the abbreviations are printed in italics so that they are emphasized. They are never printed in italics in your written text. But this stricture does not apply to any Latin tags or foreign phrases you may use: *vis-a-vis, vide ut supra, locus citatus, cela va sans dire, flagrante delicto* and any other little fancy ornaments you feel you cannot do without must always be shown in italics. However, while abbreviations are not given italics, they must, if you use them, have stops after each letter.

Breaking new ground
6.65 Although I condemn fly-by-night fashions and euph-

emisms, to say nothing of ugly neologisms and euphuistic jargon, it would be wrong to say that writers should be afraid of using new-minted words that fill a gap; provided that they do so in the right place and at the right time, they can add to their descriptive power by doing so. We have already acquired *filibuster* and *stone-walling* from the States. Australia has given us *walkabout* and a useful verb, *to whinge.* Other words are waiting to join them; *to finagle, potlatch, to sashay, boxwallah, jerkwater, high-tailing, boondocks* and *to run lickety-split.* Obviously these words have no place in a formal text, nor am I suggesting that you ought to use them. However, sometimes a word with a special descriptive impact is needed and words can be found. Don't fall into a habit of using such unorthodox words. Surprise soon disappears and you will have blunted the word.

6.66 Breaking new ground can be very tempting. To use a word in an unusual way is something that needs caution. Be sure that your new application will be fully understood. Ask yourself if you are diminishing the currently-accepted use. If you try your hand at invention, the result must be worth the risk and the word must be so right for its purpose that it will mean to others what it does to you. Innovators are not always appreciated. The hearthrug Homer, dreaming of adventure, is admired by his dog and no one else. The probable fate of your new word is to languish in the local jargon of your field of discipline or your workplace. The reason why writers acquire and improve their vocabulary is not the single-handed reform of current usage, but communication.

Words and users
6.67 If you are an engineer, a lawyer, a teacher or an aspiring author, it is certain that you will have to write something which will be read by someone other than your indulgent aunt. You enter the marketplace when you write something for others to read and the words you choose are the means by which you present your wares. No idea, opinion or theory that is badly expressed will get as much attention as one that is well written in words that make it absolutely clear and comprehensible. But English contains a vast number of

words; you have the advantage of choice and you can also choose to reflect your own individuality. The words on the paper should be *your* words and not ones dictated by someone else or picked at random.

Imagery

6.68   Whatever descriptive words or phrases you choose to illustrate a point, it is almost certain that someone has used them before. With some thousand years or so, the parts of any language have come in for a good deal of handling. Some have been handled to excess; their edges are blunted and surfaces quite worn away. They have become clichés or what Fowler calls 'battered ornaments'. Stay clear of any time-worn images which have totally lost their impact.

6.69   Imagery is a valuable tool in making a thing unseen become clear to the reader. The words 'blackheart cherry' run with blood-red juice. Homer's 'wine-dark sea' is that dark Aegean sea of a blue so intense one could drown by looking at it. A man born South of the Mason-Dixon line is using a simile when he tells you that in a friend's house 'the whisky ran like glue'. Thomas Jefferson included this metaphor when he wrote a letter to a fellow revolutionary in 1787:

> The tree of liberty must be refreshed from time to time with the blood of patriots and tyrants. It is its natural manure.

Henry James used an analogy when he wrote of the 'time-honoured bread-sauce of happy endings'.

6.70   Images and metaphors are meant to bring a picture or thought as sharply as possible to the reader's eye or consciousness. It is difficult to find new images in the old clothes of a much-used language. Newness, however, is less important than freshness of application. The image must open the mind's eye suddenly or persuasively.

6.71   The use of imagery and simile is just as important to the technical or academic writer as it is to the poet. The intention of both is to produce the right picture in the reader's mind. A description of soldiers advancing over rough terrain to new positions is none the worse for telling us that they were like a column of ants straggling along a trail of honey. Here is an earwig, feeding:

> It used its mouthparts like a knife and fork. With the teeth and sharp edges of the upper mandibles it made cuts across the stalk. Then the cut part was dug out neatly by the lower mandible and pushed into the mouth.

The insect is a poacher on a stalk of celery, but the words are the sort used to describe a man eating a steak, an action familiar to most readers. The more remote or abstruse the machine, process or state is from ordinary experience, the more necessary it is to provide a parallel image on which the reader's attention can fasten.

6.72 Wishing to describe something sharp, you might choose between, for argument's sake, *sharp as a needle, sharp as a knife* and *sharp as broken glass*. Choice depends on the type or degree of sharp sensation you want to convey. The point of a needle *punctures* or *pierces*; a knife is a weapon or tool that *cuts, slices* or *chops*; broken glass has jagged edges that suggest *slashing* or *wounding*, deliberate or accidental.

6.73 Movement can be silent, seen but not heard, like a train watched through a window, a fly crawling up the wall or an inching caterpillar. The orb-web spider, to avoid being caught on the sticky trapping threads in the web, picks its way along the 'walkways' with delicate deliberation. Movement can also be visualized through the sound it makes; you can see the movement of a beam engine or the 'nodding donkey' pump when you think of the sound. Natural history films made in elephant seal colonies showed a very particular way of getting about: the bull seal rears his blubbery weight up on his foreflippers, making himself the shape of an enormous and excessively ripe banana. His head is held high and back, no doubt to avoid treading on his nose, a sort of short trunk like a discarded wartime gasmask. To move forward, he curves his body and hitches his four to five tons of fat and loose skin along in a series of thundering bounces, each time letting out a loud gusty sigh. It is as if a steam locomotive moved its front bogie up and down in time with the puffs of steam – a sort of thump-and-belch progression. Traction engines, motorbikes and brewers' drays move in ways that can be described in terms of both sight and sound. The watchword for all descriptive phrases, however, is brevity. A short phrase, even a single word, should be able to do all the work. You must therefore regard the two descriptions, the orb-web spider and the elephant seal, as poor examples. You should also take care never to use the same image more than once in the same piece. Even a vivid and lively image loses its value in repetition.

6.74 Using colour in imagery can be difficult. Each individual sees colour and reacts to it in a different way. If you must use colour in a description and it is important for the reader to visualize it, use natural colours: the sky, spring and autumn leaves, limestone, chalk and peat. Even if the colour actually seen varies from person to person, the relationship between natural colours will be much the same. Colours have associations with emotions, moods and states of mind. It is worth bearing this in mind; some people feel colours very strongly and find that they symbolize things like the days of the week and times of year. You cannot depend on a particular reaction.

6.75 Analogy is useful in describing process and action. For example the elbow and the knee are ginglymoid joints; they work in two directions only, back and forth, in contrast to the ball-and-socket joints. Don't seize on the word *ginglymus*; the reader would have to look it up and the point of your description would be lost. On the other hand, *hinge-like* describes the limits of movement very neatly.

6.76 The purpose of imagery and analogy is to bring the thing described to the reader as clearly and effectively as possible. One good sharp image is worth a wealth of adjectives. Keep it under control, however; too much of a good thing produces satiety.

Style – The Art of Writing

6.77   A prose style is something particular to the writer's self, as personal as taste in music and food. It expresses something about the writer that belongs to no one else. That is not to say that every writer's style is good, only that it is his or hers, whether it is dull or imaginative, dry or vital.

6.78   The subject is determined, the limits are set and the shape of the work has been decided. When ideas and exposition are all down on paper the writer edits and refines the work. At this point grammar, sentence construction, idiom vocabulary and description are all in use. It is to this compound that the writer gives his or her personal characteristics.

6.79   There is more to writing than mere correctness. It must make sense and, ideally, should arouse interest, each sentence making the reader want to read the next sentence. I am not suggesting that an entire text should consist of sentences that trigger responses in the reader but rather that it should not be entirely dull. The variety of expressive modes that can be used in English have a foundation in English literature. The person who has read widely has been exposed to this variety and can gain from it. Wide reading means the exploration of a range of published work, not just a narrow band forbiddingly described as 'classics'. As much can be learnt from what is badly written (what not to do) as from elegant prose; and as yesterday's models can often be seen today as colourless, longwinded, diffuse or gaudy, so we can make personal judgements about what is to be emulated.

6.80   While you can model your style closely on the work of another writer, it is a poorhanded thing to do. Read as much as you can, but express your thoughts in a way which is natural to you. An educated adult, fluent in the English tongue, needs no master. For all that, there are good examples to study. You can learn much from other writers about the effective use of words, the value of adjectival economy, and simple and subtle sentence construction. Their style may not be yours but you can see how a subject is brought into life, how the reader's attention is directed and how the flow of thought is maintained.

6.81 The popular musical based on *The Once and Future King, Camelot*, may have distracted attention from the non-fiction work of T.H. White. When he was 30, he wrote *England Have My Bones*, more a diary than an autobiography, and an unashamedly chauvinist panegyric on English life. Here he complains about the effects of industrial development on his contemporaries:

> All truly good and great men are interested in laying and lighting fires. With mature consideration and plenty of time to examine the problem in all its aspects (scientific, architectural, thermal, physico-chemical and artistic) the noble man can light any fire with one match, so that it not only keeps burning, but begins to burn maturely quite soon.

He wants to teach this basic skill to his intellectual friends:

> The acolyte would take a pride in fetching his own coal from the cellar (without falling downstairs, stunning himself with the coal hammer, or losing his way) and in getting his hands properly black – no gloves, tongs or mush. He would light, with one match, his first real fire. How he would wait, with nervousness and trepidation, for those few seconds whilst the kindling fell in and the architecture reconstructed itself! But all would be well. The flames would falter, yellow and heatless, like little kittens; would catch hold evenly and take heart with life.
>
> T.H. White: *England Have My Bones.* Collins (1936)

6.82 Alfred Duggan wrote a number of historical novels and historical biographies in a style so engagingly simple that the reader is unaware of the formidable scholarship that lies behind it. His is the purest narrative style:

> If Tigranes had acceded to so brusque a demand so brusquely expressed he would have impaired the prestige which was his greatest asset. In public audience he was bound to refuse, though he tried to indicate that the question was not finally closed by sending magnifi-

cent presents to the lodgings of the embassy. Claudius chose to regard these courtesies as an attempt to bribe him. He returned the presents and himself went back to Cilicia, having demonstrated his fearless republican spirit by bringing about a quite unnecessary war.

Alfred Duggan: *He Died Old.* Faber, 1958

6.83   Relating events which have happened before (but are relevant to) the main thread of a narrative calls for economy. Thomas Love Peacock can put a life history into three clauses in this extract from *Nightmare Abbey.* He could be described as a romantic satirist; certainly his novels are written with a mixture of detachment and humour. Perhaps the sort of mordancy displayed here may seem out of place in a report or thesis, but one can be too solemn, and Peacock was a man who dealt with official documents as Chief Examiner at the East India Company; it is hard to believe that he could keep this sort of pungent neatness out of all his work.

Mr and Mrs Hilary brought with them an orphan niece, a daughter of Mr Glowry's youngest sister, who had made a runaway love-match with an Irish officer. The lady's fortune disappeared in the first year: love, by a natural consequence, disappeared in the second: the Irishman himself, by a still more natural consequence, disappeared in the third.

Thomas Love Peacock: *Nightmare Abbey* (1818)

6.84   Simplicity of style, like that of Thomas Love Peacock, T.H. White and Alfred Duggan is achieved by rigorous self-discipline and editing. Everything that is not essential is stripped away, yet their work is neither bare nor dull. The ease with which the English language is manipulated brings many writers down. More and yet more elegant ways of phrasing sentences present themselves. But the essence of communication is understanding. If readers must grope for meaning through involved sentences, elliptically-presented ideas or hedges of conditional clauses, you will lose them. The place for obscurity is the window-blind or curtain factory, not on paper.

6.85 Nonetheless, there are times when information should be delivered little by little. If you are establishing a scene, building up a background of events or producing a portrait, you may need to slow down the reader's pace. In these circumstances, literary devices may be useful. Antithesis sharpens the contrast between different arguments, sentiments or characteristics. Thackeray uses it to display the elements of a complex character:

> If mere parsimony could have made a man rich, Sir Pitt Crawley might have become very wealthy – if he had been an attorney in a country town, with no capital but his brains, it is very possible that he would have turned them to good account and might have achieved for himself a very considerable influence and competency. But he was unluckily endowed with a good name and a large though encumbered estate, both of which went to injure rather than advance him. He had a taste for law, which cost him many thousands yearly; and being a great deal too clever to be robbed, as he said, by any single agent, allowed his affairs to be mismanaged by a dozen, whom he all equally mistrusted. He was such a sharp landlord, that he could hardly find any but bankrupt tenants; and such a close farmer as to grudge almost the seed to the ground, whereupon vengeful Nature grudged him the crops which she granted to more liberal husbandmen. . . . As he would not pay honest agents at his granite quarry, he had the satisfaction of finding that four overseers ran away and took fortunes with them to America. . . . In disposition he was sociable and far from proud . . . he was never known to give away a shilling or do a good action, but was of a pleasant, sly, laughing mood, and would cut his joke and drink his glass with a tenant and sell him up the next day; or have his laugh with the poacher he was transporting with equal good humour.
>
> W.M. Thackeray: *Vanity Fair* (1848)

Thackeray, writing in an age when length was a means of attracting readers, could afford to catalogue his character in merciless detail. Indeed, he needed to do so, for the custom was for books to be read aloud to the family in the evenings, chapter by chapter. The nature or essence of any character had to be very firmly established so that hearers could still identify it after an interval of time and without recourse to previous pages.

6.86   Parenthetic insertions also reduce the pace of reading. Norman Douglas builds a picture slowly, phrase on phrase, clause on clause, making a large heap of dust in a dry landscape intensely alive and mysterious. Norman Douglas began his working life as a diplomat. He was a distinguished writer about travel and places, although best known for his richly funny, strange novel, *South Wind,* He could draw as vivid a picture of life in a strange land as a documentary film, using an unsentimental gift for seeing things as they really are. In this excerpt he describes phosphate deposits mined in Tunisia:

> Here they lie, the quintessential relics of those little Eocene fishes and other sea beasts, if such they were, that swam and crawled about the waters many years ago – piled up on the terraces so high that the mind grows dizzy at contemplating their multitudes or the ages required to squeeze them into this priceless powder; piled up for 500 miles along their old sea beach – an arid inland chain of hills nowadays, where hardly a blade of grass will grow; sterile themselves, the cause of surprising fertility elsewhere. These phosphates are something of a symbol: there are men and women fashioned after this model.
> Norman Douglas: *Fountains in the Sand* (1912)

6.87   There are writers who adopt a style so unsuited both to their subject and to their readers that one wonders how they achieved publication.

> Perhaps the best Morality of which we know the author's name is *Magnificence,* by John Skelton. But, especially after *Everyman*, it is dull reading for little people, and it is not in order to speak of this play that I write about John Skelton.
> H.E. Marshall: *English Literature for Boys and Girls* (1909)

Bang! Crash! Tinkle! Pop! Having unwarrantably assumed literary knowledge on the part of his audience, he proceeds to patronize them as 'little people', tells them that the play he has mentioned is dull and ends by saying that the title he has just gone on about has nothing to do with what he wants to say.

6.88 Learn to re-read your work objectively and cultivate self-awareness. All writers use tricks; but tricks only succeed if they are not spotted by the reader. It is easy to fall into a habit of using the same construction again and again and it is just as easy for the reader to learn to see them coming. Elaborately convoluted sentences, always beginning with the same, or the same sort of, word; emphasis by the repetition of a word within the same clause or sentence; an over-use of antithetic clauses: these are habits that writers must see for themselves and weed out at the editing stage. Some expressions have been so favoured for years that the writer is no longer aware of using them. Here is a lover of inverted sentences, a habit possibly acquired through lecturing students. The three sentences that follow are in consecutive paragraphs.

> Very singular are the reasonings used by which the necessity and divine right of the Empire are proved out of the Bible.

and

> More attractive to the mystical spirit than these direct arguments were those drawn from prophecy, or based on the allegorical interpretation of Scripture.

Here he hitches up his gown and marches back and forth:

> Very early in Christian history had the belief formed itself that the Roman Empire – as the fourth beast of Daniel's vision, as the iron legs and feet of Nebuchadnezzar's image – was to be the world's last and universal kingdom.
>
> James Bryce: *The Holy Roman Empire* (1890)

6.89   Make direct statements wherever possible. If you are not certain of your facts, write nothing until you have done some more work and checked them. If what you want to say is conjecture or opinion, make it clear that it is your own idea and get on with the statement. Handwringing apologies like *Some people are of the opinion that* . . . ; or *It could be supposed* . . . ; or *It is felt in some quarters* . . . are annoying to read. If the writer thinks a thing is so, he must say so; he has no business hiding his personal opinions from the reader with that sort of smoke-screen. The sideways shuffle into a sentence is also very tiresome: *It may be of some interest* (which means that it is of no interest whatever); *I should like to mention in passing* (as you are going to mention it anyway there is no need to lick your lips over it); *Let us take into consideration* (the reader will consider it if he or she wants to. You don't have to pretend to be the reader's chum).

6.90   If you include dialogue, reporting words exactly as they were said, make sure that the reader is never in doubt about the speaker's identity. One well-known novelist goes in for pages of unattributed conversation at a time; it is like a tape-recording of a tennis match in which the shots are described but the players never named. The reader has to keep counting the remarks to identify the speaker. Never be afraid of *he said* and *she said*. If necessary, in a long series of short speeches, you can use the occasional variation: *said X, she questioned* or *the grandfather grumbled*. Don't carry it too far; *pouted, whined, cried, smiled* or *howled* can be more tiresome than repetitions of *said*. In non-fiction, indirect speech (5.55) is always to be preferred as a text broken by quotation marks is less attractive to the eye.

6.91   Adjust your style to suit your reader. It is all too easy to tell a favourite aunt that you cannot come to tea, but it is surprising how many otherwise competent people make a dog's breakfast of replying to an invitation in the third person. Aunt will be sorry to hear that your gout is troubling you. On the other hand, the unfortunate secretary of the institute or body giving a formal reception or dinner has not the slightest interest in the birthday party or sun-drenched beach which will prevent you from accepting. He or she only wants to know how many chops or bottles of Ruritanian burgundy will be needed. The necessary information has to appear in the first line without frills or explanations:

> Mr X regrets that he is unable to accept the kind invitation of . . .

or

> Ms W accepts with pleasure the kind invitation of . . .

6.92 Reports are often unwieldy things, overloaded with detail and explanation. They need not be. Here is a wartime accident report that condenses everything into a neat, straightforward statement:

> Officer Commanding – – – Squadron
>
> Damage to Hampden – – –
>
> On – – – –, 1941, I was the captain of Hampden aircraft – – – –, in operations over – – – –. We met some flak but did not seem to have been damaged. We landed normally at base but, while taxying to dispersal, the port engine fell off.
>
> I have the honour to be, Sir
>
> Your obedient servant
>
> – – – –   – – – – , Pilot Officer.

6.93 If we look back to the 17th century, we can find two writers, with styles utterly different from each other, who share a capacity for the uncompromising search for the right word and the right measure for what they wish to say. John Bunyan's rhythm is much that of the King James version of the Bible; *Pilgrim's progress* is a dialogue, delivered in short sentences and plain speech. It is also a work of faith, an allegory, told as a dream. In this speech Faithful is telling Christian what happened to him after he left the house of Adam the First:

So soon as the man overtook me, he was but a word and a blow, for down he knocked me, and laid me for dead. But when I was a little come to myself again, I asked him wherefore he served me so. He said, because of my secret inclining to Adam the First: and with that he struck me another deadly blow on the breast, and beat me down backward; so I lay at his foot as dead as before. So, when I came to myself again, I cried him mercy; but he said, I know not how to show mercy; and with that knocked me down again. He had doubtless made an end of me, but that one came by, and bid him forbear.

The tranquil philosopher, Sir Thomas Browne, unfolds his thoughts slowly. This little passage could be set to music:

But Seeds themselves do lie in perpetual shades, either under the leaf, or shut up in coverings; and such as lye barest, have their husks, skins and pulps about them, wherein the nebbe and generative particle lyeth moist and secured from the injury of ayre and Sunne. Darknesse and light hold interchangeable dominions, and alternately rule the seminal state of things.

Sir Thomas Browne: *The Garden of Cyrus*

Those two examples are voices from the past. Their styles are not usable as models today; rather it is their skill with words that one must try to match. The difficulty that the student of literature finds is that the great men of the past have little in common with today's writers. Coleridge, Hazlitt, Charles Lamb, De Quincey and Ruskin wrote essays and dissertations which found a ready readership. If a writer wished to carry on about a pet subject he could count on finding someone who wanted to read about it.

6.94 Most non-fiction nowadays is severely practical. It is often informative, a means of putting other people in touch with work that has been done in a particular field, a working description of a process or a relation of events, mistakes or profits. Many books written by professional people for others in their profession adopt an informal style, though informality has to be very well done to succeed. They could do worse than study how Henry Kingsley, an under-rated writer, achieves a direct approach to the reader. Using short, easy sentences, he manages to simulate a conversational rhythm, as if the reader were in the same room. In this extract, he shares an experience, as with a friend, rather than just describing how one should deal with a sleepless night.

> When you are going to have a night of this kind, you seldom know it beforehand, for certain. Sometimes, if you have had much experience in the sort of thing – if you have lost money, or gone in debt, or if your sweetheart has cut you very often – you may at least guess, before you get your boots off, that you are going to have a night of it; in which case, read yourself to sleep *in bed.* Never mind burning the house down (that would be rather desirable as a distraction from thought); but don't read till you are sleepy with your clothes on, and then undress, because, if you do, you will find, by the time you have undressed yourself that you are terribly awake and, when the candle is blown out, you will be all ready for a regular Walpurgis night.
>
> Henry Kingsley: *Ravenshoe* (1862)

6.95 To provide a reader with a clear picture of a piece of equipment or machinery seems, for some writers, very difficult. Because they know so much about it themselves, they are unable to get down to first principles and put it together piece by piece, so to speak, for someone else. Here is a description of a cotton press, as used in Virginia before the War between the States, that is crystal-clear:

> To work the press a mule walked around and around in a sixty-foot circle, hitched to one end of a revolving pair of oblique timbers, joined above like a pair of calipers. These were balanced at their union on the summit of an immense wooden screw, eighteen inches in diameter outside the threads, and threaded for a distance of twelve or fifteen feet. The nut through which this big screw descended was held up, twelve or fifteen feet above the ground, by immense timbers, and in itself

consisted of four whiteoak sections, two feet square and ten feet long. These four timbers were held together by ten- or twelve-inch square hickory and whiteoak braces and black locust wedges. When the big screw came slowly down, revolved by a sprightly mule, 500 pounds of cotton could easily be compressed into a standard bale.

Paul Barringer: *The Natural Bent* (1949)

6.96 Emotion alone cannot produce good writing. Strong emotion distorts prose and is the enemy of style. Anger, indignation, even grief, need to be tempered if the full import is to reach the reader. Take time to balance your-self. Most people are made incoherent by rage, so, if you are burning to let loose with a polemic, diatribe or animadversion, sleep on it. You will feel better in the morning and be ready to produce more subtle and telling arguments.

6.97 Style is a process of combination; considering the reader; yet maintaining a personal manner of expression; pro-ducing balanced, readable sentences; and making expression vivid and alive – all polished by self-criticism. Dr Johnson's tutor told him that if he thought he had written something particularly fine, he should strike it out. You need not go quite so far; it is enough to avoid falling in love with your own work.

Chapter Seven
Unseen partners–the readers

7.1   The simplest piece of writing is an intellectual exercise; it requires thought. Reports, legal opinions, complaints to the laundry, theses and examination answers are the product of that thought. Up to this point concentration has been on the nuts and bolts and the building of the model. Clearly there is more to making a bicycle than the random assembly of components; the intention is to make a rideable machine. In making it, moreover, the use to which it is to be put is an essential consideration. It would be futile to spend time making a child's tricycle if you plan to take part in the Tour de France. You must think about the purpose towards which you are directing effort.

7.2   The first principle is that it takes two to communicate. Water Boards do not fill reservoirs for their own satisfaction; at the other end of their work is a householder turning on a tap. A funny story loses its savour if there is no listener. The haberdashery is there, not because the haberdasher takes pleasure in stockpiling socks, but to sell socks to customers. To succeed with a consumer, whether of water, jokes or socks, you must envisage the real person, study needs, reactions and tastes, Those who write for themselves alone are not communicating. They are writing diaries.

7.3   Writers write for readers and the proper study for authors is the audience for whom they write. Fiction aside, there are three main categories of readers: those who know more than you do; those who know as much; and those who know less or nothing at all about your subject.

7.4   The reader who is more knowledgeable than you are presents a challenge. You must convince such a reader that you have acquired the level of knowledge expected of you. If this were just a matter of handing back gobbets of information in the same condition in which you received them, it would need only the effort of getting them down on paper. However a tape recorder would perform as well and the reader would be entitled to think you intellectually un-impressive, even though you have a good memory.

7.5 The task is to convince that reader that you have digested what you have received and can make use of it. There is no need to catch the reader's attention; for better or worse, he or she is committed to reading your stuff. Make sure that material is presented in the right logical sequence: first things first. Trim off tempting frills and flights of fancy. Good structure is the essential requirement. Showing off by larding the text with polysyllables is self-defeating. Use only the technical terms that are absolutely necessary; the reader knows them all and won't be impressed. A dental student told me that he used the word *traumatized* rather than *bruised* 'because it sounded more professional'. What he described was a perfectly ordinary bruise and *trauma* was too elaborate a word for it. Stick to the barest word that will show your grasp of the subject.

7.6 If you are very confident in your knowledge of the subject and feel that you have already outrun your mentors in their own field, never let it show. Show a proper deference to age and seniority. The head of your department may have a profound knowledge of the over-confident know-all and the head that has grown too big for its hat.

7.7 Never, ever, quote from work that has not been discussed during term if it goes counter to what has been taught. If it is worth your attention it can wait until your academic subservience is done. No one will stop you from keeping notes of your own on opinions you think worth pursuing; but cultivate humility until the certificate or degree is yours.

7.8 In writing for one's peers, there is temptation. Some-times, instead of sharing information or entering new ground, one is offered an opportunity to demolish someone's work or ideas. Floorwiping is fun but not a good idea. Using another person as a dishclout can produce a triumphant little thrill; it also makes enemies and everyone needs friends. Even if one is strongly in disagreement with the opinions of others, one should regard it as a measure of skill to state this tactfully as well as firmly.

7.9 It may seem a waste of effort to give colleagues or the members of your own coterie the courtesy of well-written prose. If so, it is a pity. Lucid exposition, with ideas, theories or opinions well set out can only increase the esteem of those who are on your side and impress those who don't know you, while confounding your enemies. Don't forget that someone else may derive great satisfaction from picking holes in your work.

7.10 The jargon of your discipline or industry is that in-language used to describe states, processes or equipment that may have perfectly sound names already. To indulge in it on all occasions is a slovenly habit. It is not just the factory-floor slang or laboratory lingo that counts as jargon. Jargon also includes all those pompous phrases which may have seemed so clever the first time they were used and the ponderous orismology of new disciplines, their tread getting dangerously low as they are trundled out again and again. Reading articles and texts written by educationists and psychologists, one is amazed at the amount of verbiage their fellow educationists and psychologists are prepared to munch through to get at the small kernels of real information. It is off-hand, not to say offensive, to treat colleagues, members of the same department or scientists in the same discipline to the same sort of thought-concealing piffle that is handed out to an ignorant public.

7.11 The reader who most deserves the writer's attention is the one who can be supposed to know less about the subject than the author. The aim, in writing for such a reader, may be to inform, to explain, to educate, to sell or to entertain. In the context of this book, information, explanation and education are the most probable aims, but entertainment cannot be ignored. How are the other aims to be achieved if the reader is bored? The reader is sold the ideas by making them palatable and agreeable. Presentation is a crucial element in any exchange between author and reader. Clarity is just as important; if readers can't understand what is written, writers waste their efforts.

7.12   Having taken a vow to present facts attractively and clearly you must identify your reader. Don't point your work in the wrong direction. Hitting the gold in someone else's target doesn't merit a score. No one writes for all the world; even journalists consider the nature of their paper's readership. There may be one particular category – members of an occupational group, for example – to whom you have something to say. Are you going to keep within narrow limits or do you hope that people outside those limits may also be interested? The message that has to be taken to heart is that writers must know for whom they write; if they do not, nobody else will, including readers.

7.13   Remind yourself of the styles which most irritate you. People do not read books in order to be patronized, though this is often their fate. A note of patronage makes the reader feel despised by the author, who may have intended no such thing. On the other hand, it can give an impression that an author is not wholly certain of the subject. Trying too hard for simplicity can create a picture of looking down from Olympian heights; if the content is watered down too much the readers feel diminished. They are not to know that the author is not really arrogant, only incapable.

7.14   Waggishness and facetious forms of presentation put readers' backs up and divert their attention. Many find an assumption of mateyness offensive. An uninvited circular came through my door advertising a journal 'that is deliberately intended for a group of executives who need their business news in a unique format'. The signer of the letter (his signature was printed in blue so that I could deceive myself into believing it to be hand-written) goes on to tell me that he believes 'that you are a member of this group and that only – – – – can meet your particular news requirements'. I was affronted because this stranger had assumed certain things about me, none of which were true.

7.15   An anthropomorphic approach to explanation can be a hazardous choice. There are people who have a natural anti-pathy to the attribution of human qualities to inanimate objects. Not all children liked stories of talking balloons and adventurous steamrollers; it is an assumption that, as adults, they still abhor fantasy. If it serves the purpose of clarification, use the animal world as a source of analogy, but keep descriptions of equipment and machinery in technical work firmly neuter and impersonal.

7.16 Impressing the reader by wallowing in scientific or technical information is counter-productive. It is often the result of an author's inability to put him or herself in the reader's place. The reader sees someone who would rather be admired than understood. If a man is trying to sell another an ice-cream cornet, he would be ill-advised to harp on the non-milk fat content and the means of extruding the product from the processing vat. Instead he will tell the customer of its delicious flavour and enticing texture. So the customer is brought to believe that he will enjoy it and pays his money. A sales executive will never sell a sausage, still less a complex piece of equipment, if he confuses the customer. The engineer whose specifications are a bewildering mass of technicalities is a liability to his firm. The technical term is seldom necessary for understanding; doctors do not have to tell patients that they are *pyrexic* when they have a fever.

7.17 Readers, then, are to be regarded as rational, intelligent human beings who can take in information, be they members of your own profession, customers, students or laymen. It follows that the content of your work must always be determined by your readership. If the reader is clearly in your mind, address yourself to that person. It is not enough to write yards of explanation and tons of information. It must be as direct a communication as it is when you write a letter to someone you know.

7.18 Bear in mind the origins of the work as well as its reader. The editor, publisher or head of department may have an influence on what you write and how you write it. Although Chapter Two dealt with the mechanical process of writing things down, it is worth looking at the subject again. There may be constraints that you will have to watch. Some companies and Government Departments want reports set out according to a pattern. Journals often specify length. Part of your work may involve a chronological sequence of events while another part is concerned with interpretation or comparison. The decisions you make about ordering your text depend first on the constraints mentioned earlier and secondly, and more importantly, on what the reader needs to be told and in what order and style it will best make sense.

7.19 Review the text as you go, taking care that the reader will seldom have to refer to other pages. If there are many terms that need definition, include a glossary. However, putting in a glossary does not excuse you from defining the term when it first occurs in the text.

7.20 Make sure that maps and diagrams are as close as possible to their text references and do not use tables unless they will really help the reader. Tables and graphs chop up a text and the reader is forced to rabbit back and forth between the table and the flow of print on which attention should be concentrated. Stuffing paragraphs with percentages and statistics is a fashionable habit; very often a general reference to figures would be enough, with the exact figures given in an appendix for readers who have a passion for accurate numbers. Watch the structural formulae in chemistry texts; it is absolutely necessary for the author to mark bonds in pencil. If they are not marked the printer may mistake them for ordinary rules and use an em-rule instead of the one for the purpose, or you could find that all your bonds have become en-rules. Give thought, too, to the number of structural formulae you want to include; use only those that are really needed; structural formulae are artwork and must be separately drawn. This is not only expensive – it also takes time. It is important to use SI units of measurements, as the Royal Society recommends. If you feel that you must use another system, this should be made clear to the reader at the start of the work.

7.21 These strictures apply to biologists as well. Biochemists in the fields of Microbiology, Bacteriology, Nuclear

Biology and Molecular Engineering (there are many more subdivisions) must be careful about nomenclature; even within these disciplines there is often disagreement about terminology. They confuse the issue more by using, for example, Greek letters in a variety of founts to mean different things. Worse, the use to which Greek letters are put by one branch of Biology is quite different from the uses of other branches and of Chemistry. The reader may be faced with a Greek character (γ), gamma in roman or *gamma* in italic; as these have different meanings in different branches of science, the writer must proclaim the ground rules before starting on the text. Remember that all programmes, other than *computer programs*, are spelt with two *m*'s and an *e*. Keep spelling and presentation consistent throughout your work.

7.22 Unless there is a good reason not to do so, keep the thread of concentration going by presenting things in a logical sequence, especially processes and functions. When giving an account of equipment, if a new item is mentioned, it must be described. If you tell someone that a pump-up alarm* is part of the system and it has not appeared in the text before you must tell him what it is.

7.23 Certain readers must be considered very carefully. These are the decision-makers. Without their authority recommendations will not be carried out; they may allocate physical resources; or they may hold the purse strings. For all their importance, they may have little technical or scientific knowledge with which to evaluate your work. You can expect them to have technical advisers or to seek the opinion of qualified persons. Nevertheless if these are the readers to whom you first address yourself your text must be suited to their needs.

7.24 Some years ago there was an International Conference for Researchers. They were all employed by Government

---

*A pump-up alarm is one that depends on continuity to sound. The electric current, voltage or compressed air that keeps it silent must be kept at a constant level of voltage or pressure or the alarm will sound.

Departments in their own countries to improve standards in their fields. Rather surprisingly, the purpose of the Conference was not, as one might suppose, to share the products of research. These researchers had met to find a solution to a shared problem: although they did what was asked of them by their Government masters, their recommendations were never put into practice. They had come together to find out why this was so and what could be done about it. Paper after paper was read. The researchers complained that their work was ignored in their homelands, and they pondered the possibilities of psychological profiles, of lack of understanding, of an unwillingness to pay more than lip-service to the question of improvements and many more reasons. Unfortunately, the papers showed beyond doubt why their work was not taken seriously. They expressed themselves with a pompous ferocity; sentences were served up with a collection of barbarous neologisms that should have made them blush with shame. Pseudo-scientific terms were borrowed from philosophy, mathematics, telecommunications, electronic engineering, even from biology and geology. The policy-makers and decision-takers of whom they complained must, over the years, have been stupefied by the outpourings they received. Far from being impressed by this mumbo-jumbo, they had thrown all the recommendations into the waste-paper basket. At the end of the Conference it had become apparent that members of the same discipline from different countries, and even different parts of the same country, did not use the same terminology and were often unable to understand each other. We can see why in these two statements:

> The ailment of our sciences; the lack of diachronic and synchronic coherence and consistency in our theory and conceptual production. . . .

and

> Standardization of terms should lead to a multilingual thesaurus of 'core concepts' to enable researchers also to employ the correct terminology when using another language.

This sort of object-defeating twaddle can be turned into English. The first means

> Members of our profession are incoherent and muddled in their thinking,

and the second means

> We need an intelligible universal terminology so that we can understand one another.

7.25   If your communication is intended for policy-makers or decision-takers you must let them see whether what you have to say is soundly based; whether it will work; how reliable your information is; whether your recommendations will achieve the results for which they hope; and how much it will cost. Your exposition needs to be written in a way that will let the important layman understand what is involved, but it must also be explicit enough to satisfy any technical advisers or the ultimate users to whom it may be passed for comment. If diagrams and highly technical details are needed, the text will be clearer if they are included at the end as appendixes.

7.26   For readers who have no power, but have a right to be informed, use a different approach. Explanations should be explicit, but make information credible and wholly available. Never make the reader feel that you find the act of writing or the subject dull. If it is not one that you like you must make an extra effort because boredom is a communicable disease. The writer is like an actor who must play a part opposed to his own character and must generate enthusiasm from within. Nothing is more engaging than a well-written piece on a subject that interests the writer.

Postscript
If a man tells you that he can write anything effortlessly, at the drop of a hat, then prepare to kick him downstairs. It is *not* easy to write. The writer's problem is to make a continuous product by a discontinuous process.

We often write things under stress, short of time or space; letters are written in busy offices; articles are put together without the luxury of freedom from interruption; whole books are written on the corner of the kitchen table. The writer struggles to keep the thread of continuity intact because there is no effective way of apologizing to the reader for disjointed utterance caused by disconnected time. Readers have a potent way of dealing with it; they put it in the wastepaper basket.

Even in tranquil working conditions, the business of turning thoughts into words is uneven. Like a dog dragging a leg of lamb up a hill, it is a matter of fits and starts and pauses to chew on the subject. As the climb proceeds the subject becomes less fresh and more stale, while the dog is frankly tired. Only the prospect of reaching the goal keeps things moving. This book is no exception; it represents enough paper, used in drafts, to fill a small warehouse and enough mental energy expended to keep London alight for hours. But if what you have written earns good marks, or pleases someone, or helps even a small number of readers, then you will find that the effort is worth while.

Appendix I

A List of Recommended Books

Notice how the titles are set out: first, the author's, or authors', name or names, followed by the date of publication, the title, then the place of publication and the name of the publisher. Use this system if you are ordering a book or preparing a booklist for an essay, thesis or work to be published.

Dictionaries

You must own at least one dictionary. The number of words it contains is less important than the information it gives you about words: the parts of speech to which they belong and their uses as those parts of speech; the breadth of definitions; and the prepositions, conjunctions and verb forms with which they are associated. By all means have a second dictionary to give you every word, abstruse, obscure, slang or pejorative, that can be dug up, but you still need the recommended one as your first point of grammatical reference. Choose the hardcover binding, or ask for it as a birthday present; it will last longer and you will want to consult it many times. Avoid 'pocket' dictionaries.

SYKES, J.B. (Ed), (1982): *The Concise Oxford Dictionary of Current English*, Oxford: Clarendon Press.

OXFORD ENGLISH DICTIONARY DEPARTMENT (1981): *The Oxford Dictionary for Writers and Editors*. Oxford: Clarendon Press. This is a guide to the practical aspects of writing, dealing with abbreviations, *-ize* endings, awkward or difficult spellings, the use of italics and capital letters, as well as punctuation and foreign and classical words and phrases.

Practical Grammars and Books on Usage

CAREY, G.V. (revised edition 1971): *Mind the Stop.* Harmondsworth: Penguin Books. An excellent and comprehensive guide to punctuation, this covers every nuance and construction.

CRYSTAL, D. (1984): *Who Cares About English Usage?* Harmondsworth: Penguin. Although this book deals for the most part with spoken English, it has some trenchant comments about certain common misusages, all the easier to remember because the author makes his points in an entertaining way.

FIELDHOUSE, H. (1982): *Everyman's Good English Guide.* London: J.M. Dent and Sons Ltd. Read and absorb every word of the Introduction. The author gives the reasons for aiming at good English and avoiding slipshod usage in a way that I cannot better. The book is particularly useful in listing words that cause difficulties, though the author is as much concerned with pronunciation as with misuse. The second section, headed 'Sentences', is a good quick reference for points of syntax.

FOWLER, H.W. (2nd edition 1965): *Modern English Usage.* Oxford: Clarendon Press. H.W. Fowler brought a common-sense approach and a sense of humour to his work as a prescriptive grammarian. From *Bird's-nesting* (perish the thought) to *Yahoo*, see FAUN, this book is full of good things. It is a splendid book to dip into, reading any entry that catches your eye. Try Sobriquets, Battered Ornaments, Barbarisms, Out of the Frying Pan and take to heart Unequal Yokefellows. Read the entry under *Belly*, which begins 'Belly is a good word now almost done to death by genteelism'. Unfortunately, Fowler's wit and humour mean that it is difficult to find any particular point; but every time you open it, you will stumble across something worth knowing.

FOWLER, H.W. and F.G. (revised edition 1973): *The King's English.* Oxford: Clarendon Press. This is largely concerned with syntax and gives many examples of misconstructions. You will need to know what you are looking for and consult the index.

GOWERS, E. (revised edition 1973): *The Complete Plain Words.* Harmondsworth: Pelican Books. Read this book chapter by chapter, taking it all to heart. Then use it as a reference book, though you will need to consult the index to find the answer to a problem.

PARTRIDGE, E. (revised edition 1973): *Usage and Abusage: A Guide to Good English.* Harmondsworth: Penguin Books. Set out in dictionary form, this book identifies many common mistakes and problem areas. It is very useful but you must know what you are looking for.

THOMSON, A.J. and MARTINET, A.V. (3rd edition, 1980): *A Practical English Grammar.* Oxford: Oxford University Press. Designed as a school textbook, for use with exercises, this grammar is a very handy reference book, full of examples.

TREBLE, H. and VALLINS, G.H. (1936): *An ABC of English Usage.* Oxford University Press. This is an immeasurably useful little book. The alphabetically-listed headings cover a very wide range of language-use questions. The entries have very full and lucid explanations. Search bookshops for it – it is worth almost any price asked.

WIENER, E.S.C. (1983): *The Oxford Miniguide to English Usage.* Oxford: Clarendon Press. This pocket-sized book has separate sections on derivations, pronunciation, vocabulary and grammar.

The Olympians

Many of the authorities on English grammar are not English: Professor Jespersen was Danish, Professor Sonnenschein was German; Dr Zandwoort is Dutch and Dr Friedrichsen is Scandinavian. Home-grown grammarians include the late Dr C.T. Onions and Professor Randolph Quirk. Many British authorities are described primarily as lexicographers: the Fowler brothers and Eric Partridge. There are also English language specialists and teachers, professional and amateur, among them G.H. Vallins, Sir Ernest Gowers and Wilfred Whitton (John O'London). The Linguistics specialists command more attention than grammarians today: Professor Palmer, Noam Chomsky, H.A. Gleason, David Crystal and many others. These are very rough-and-ready categories; many might be regarded as professing both Linguistics and Grammar, while lexicographers are often prescriptive grammarians and probably have the greatest impact on written English. Certainly they offer more practical help to the writer.

Scholarly works on English grammar and usage are very necessary though they seem to try to find order in disorder, to make English fit into a neat, predictable framework or to search for reasons to match practice. With many irregularities of form and function discovering pattern is almost impossible; the best we can do is to educate our eyes and ears, and to develop a feeling for what is right and mellifluous. If we had to pursue a thorough study of English grammar before putting pen to paper, we should never find time to write. Nevertheless, the book you are reading is no more than a simplified introduction and you should take the opportunity to read further in the texts mentioned next – or certainly the first three.

ONIONS, C.T. (1904), revised and prepared from the author's materials, MILLER, B.D.H. (1971): *Modern English Syntax.* London: Routledge and Kegan Paul.

ZANDVOORT, R.W. (1957): *A Handbook of English Grammar.* London: Longman.

JESPERSEN, OTTO (1933): *Essentials of English Grammar.* London: George Allen and Unwin. o.p.

QUIRK, RANDOLPH (1962), 2nd edition (1968): *The Use of English.* Harlow, Essex: Longman Group.

PALMER, FRANK (1971): *Grammar.* Harmondsworth: Penguin Books.

JOOS, MARTIN (1964): *The English Verb.* Madison, Wisc: University of Wisconsin Press.

CRYSTAL, DAVID (1971): *Linguistics;* Harmondsworth: Penguin Books.

History and Development
POTTER, S. (1950): *Our Language.* Harmondsworth: Penguin Books.

VALLINS, G.H. (1956): *The Pattern of English.* Harmondsworth: Penguin Books.

BROOK, G.L. (1985): *The History of the English Language;* London: Andre Deutsch.

Special Purposes
COLLOCOTT, T.C. and DOBSON, A.B. (Eds) (1974):

Chambers Dictionary of Science and Technology. Edinburgh: Chambers.

HART, H. (37th edition 1978): *Hart's Rules for Compositors and Readers*. Oxford: Oxford University Press.

ROGET, P.M. (1852) (many later editions): *Thesaurus of English Words and Phrases*. The person who sits frozen before the typewriter, searching for an elusive word or one that avoids a repetition, will see this book as a friend. A word of warning: many words listed are related or similar in meaning, but not necessarily exactly so. The purpose of the book is to refresh your vocabulary and suggest other ways of expressing an idea. It is not a dictionary and should never be used as one. Some academics profess a snobbish attitude to the Thesaurus, claiming that no educated person should need to use it. Brush aside such petty high-mindedness; most of them probably keep their copies in plain brown paper wrappers in case anyone should suspect them of owning such a practical work.

Penguin Books publish a range of specialist dictionaries and the Oxford University Press catalogue contains some useful titles.

Appendix II

Peculiar Customs — Idiomatic Usage

Most verbs vary their prepositional partners according to the context in which they find themselves. But some marry one preposition for life and acknowledge no others. Given the wrong preposition they lose their impact and, I'm afraid, betray the writer's ignorance. Until the sense of fitness of your preposition becomes instinctive, it is worth checking in the dictionary to ensure that you have put the right partners together. Some we seldom mismatch.

List I:

laugh at	give to
think of	rely on
ask for	wait for
wish for	look at

However, because some verbs fall victim to the wrong preposition more than others, I have listed them next. A second list gives the nouns and adjectives with verbal associations that suffer the same fate.

List II:

to accompany (something) *with* (something), never *by*
to be accompanied (escorted) *by* someone, never *with*
to acquiesce *in* (something), never *to*
to adhere *to* (something), never *by*
to afflict (someone) *with* (something), never *by*
to aim at (something), never *for*
to assist (someone) *in* (doing something), never *to*
to assist *at* (a meeting, etc.)
to assist *in* (action of any kind), never *to*
to avoid - no preposition, never *from*
to be careful *of* (something), never *with*

to compare = (*estimate* similarity) *with*, never *to*
to compare = (*state* similarity) *to*, never with
to comprise - no preposition, never *of, with* or *by*
to confide (something) *to* (someone)
to confide *in* (someone)
to consist (be composed) *of* (material things)
to consist (when it means *is*) *in* - as: the work consists in filing papers; virtue consists in being uncomfortable.
to consist (harmonize) *with* - as: the form consists with the content.
to contact (neologism - use sparingly) no preposition, never *to* or *with*
to be contacted *by*
to make or be in contact *with*
to be content *with*, never *by*
to contrast (examine degree of dissimilarity) *with*, never *by* or *to*
to converse *with* (someone), never *to*
to convince (someone) *of* (something), never *to*
to deduce *from* (something), never *by*
to differ *from* (something)
to differ *with* (someone)
to differ *by* (degrees of difference)
to dispense (to give out), no preposition
to dispense (release someone or something) *from* (an obligation), never *of*
to dispense (do without) *with* (something), never *of*
to be embarrassed *by* (someone or something), never *at*
to be encumbered *with* (something), never *by*
to enforce (impose action) *upon* (someone), never *by*
to foist (something) *on* (someone), never *with*
to forbid (someone) *to* (do something), never *from*
to be ill *with* (something), never *of*
to inflict (something) *on* (someone), never *with*
to instil (something) *into* (someone, something), never *with*
to interpolate - no preposition, never *by*
to be involved *in* (something), never *by*
to judge *by* (something), never *on*
to judge *that* (something or somebody is)
to judge (suppose something to be) *from* (something)
to listen *to* (something), never *at*
to be oblivious *of* (something), never *to*

to preface *with* (something), never *to*
to prefix to (something), never *by* or *with*
to protest *against* (something), never *at*
to be sensible *of*, never *to*
to be sensitive *to*, never *of*
to be solicitous (desirous) *of* (something), never *to*
to be solicitous *to* (do something)
to be solicitous *about* (someone)
to be sparing *of* (something), never *with*
to suffer *from* (illness), never *with*
to be superior *to*, never *than*
to talk *to* (someone), never *with*
to be tolerant *of*, never *to*
to be unconscious *of*, never *to*

List III:

Nouns, adjectives and adverbs needing specific prepositions.
adherence (noun) *to* (someone, something)
adherent (noun) *of* (someone's)
adverse (adj.) (Hostile or injurious) *to*, never *from*
averse (adj.) *to*
aversion (noun) *to*
aversive (adj.) (jargon term, use only inside discipline)
comparison (noun) *in – – – – with* (something), never *to*
contrast (noun) *in – – – – to* (something), never *with*
different (adj.) *from*, never *to* or *than*
　　It is always better to be different *from*. After all you would not
　　write 'bread differs *to* cake'.
experience (noun) (to have) – – – *of* (a subject)
experienced (verbal adj.) *in* (a subject)
inferior *to*, never *than*
knowledge (noun) *of* (something)
knowledgeable (adj.) *about* (something)
receptive (adj.) *of* (something), never *to*
sensible, see List II
sensitive, see List II
sympathy (noun) *with* or *for* (someone), never *to*

superior (adj.) *to*, never *than*
tolerant (adj.) *of*, never *to*

In addition to the notional words that are choosy about the prepositions they take, there are others which are idiomatically followed by a particular verb form. Some have to precede an infinitive; others always go before *to* and a gerund. Obviously they can't all be listed here. The range of such words is wide and the sense of the right verb form to use depends on developing a feeling for the peculiarities of the English language. If you use the dictionary recommended in Appendix I, you will find some guidance. It must be searched for, however, as the definitions indicate the correct verb form by one example and do not set it out as clearly as they do the prepositions. Here are words followed by the *wrong* verb form.

He admits to have misjudged the issue;
Dr Bugwinder succeeded to achieve his goal;
There is a tendency to allowing too much freedom;
The team announced its intention to going on with the race.

Here are lists of some idiomatic words; each word is followed by a sample of the form required.

List IA: Verbs taking the infinitive.

learn (to do)
expect (to meet)
threaten (to sue)
intend (to go)

refuse (to allow)
suffice (to convince)
tend (to corrupt)
oblige (to perform)

List IB: Verbs taking *to*, or another preposition, and the gerund.

object (to paying)
commit (passive) (to acting)
test (by examining)
mend (by repairing)
persist (in doing)
suspect (of stealing)

confess (to receiving)
succeed (in making)
prevent (from doing)
aim (at achieving)
blame (for failing)

List IIA: Nouns taking the infinitive.

determination (to succeed)
inspiration (to write)
obligation (to protect)
threat (to proceed)

refusal (to perform)
tendency (to bend)
duty (to arrest)

List IIB: Nouns and adjectives taking a preposition and gerund.

habit (of fidgeting)
intention (of declaring)
unequal (to performing)
idea (of writing)
suspicion (of forging)
objection (to agreeing)

neglect (of protecting)
equal (to doing)
plan (of composing)
object (of carrying out)
resistance (to being forced)

Distinctions of time and meaning

Using an infinitive or a gerund without a preposition, after a verb, can show a difference of time.

> I must remember to turn off the gas

is in the future, but

> I remember meeting him

is in the past. We differentiate between *try* (to attempt) and *try* (to experiment) by using an infinitive with the first:

> Try to reach agreement,

and a gerund with the second:

> She tried adding baking powder.

Deliberate intention after *begin* and *stop* is expressed by the gerund.

> Trains stopped running after midnight,

and

> I began writing my thesis.

But chance, or an unconsidered action, lies with the infinitive.

> I stopped to think what to do,

and

> It began to rain.

In written work it is always preferable to use the infinitive after *start.*

> I start to work on the experiment today

rather than

> I start working in Wokingham tomorrow.

The infinitive is more precise.

Phrasal Verbs

Idioms arise from special needs: a particular sort of action acquires its own verbal form. Certain combinations of verbs and prepositions or adverbs are used to specify the way in which something happens or is carried out. Where the combinations fit circumstances which often occur, the words in them are treated as a phrasal verb, in which the two words act as one.

The characteristic of phrasal verbs is that the verbs on which they are based have meanings of their own when used without the accompanying preposition or adverb. Sometimes the parts of the combination can be used separately in the same sentence with exactly the same meaning, though the use of the words together strengthens and reinforces the statement.

> I have decided to *give away* my cat
> I have decided to *give* my cat *away.*

Some phrasal verbs lose the specific meaning when split; others become nonsense.

> I went to *lie* on the bed *down.*
> She *gave* to his demands *in.*

Here is a list of some commonly-used phrasal verbs.

get up	make up	send away (for)	break through
lie down	put off	fill in (on)	close down
give in	put up (with)	come up (against)	flash back
give up	die away	put down (to)	line up
give away	live down	face up to	pay off
account for	follow up	do away with	print out
look for	hear of	look forward to	turn on

Some combinations are made into adjectives:

> an unlooked-for result
> an unheard-of complaint

Others have a variety of combinations:

> stand for
> stand up to
> stand up for

One, in particular, is always reflexive. I read a manuscript in which this verb, shorn of its reflexive preposition, was misused on 17 pages.

> avail (oneself) *of*

Idiomatic usage cannot be swallowed like a slow-release capsule. If it does not come naturally, then it must be learnt, example by example. The fine points of written English usage fill many large books. The ones listed in Appendix I deal only with usage for the writer. English colloquial usage is markedly different; it is not a good thing to rely on grammars produced for the foreign student. Most of the grammars published in the last few years have concentrated on helping the understanding of the spoken word. Since so much badly written English work is produced, however, from texts to reports, essays to handbooks and specifications to simple notices, it is vitally necessary to get back a standard of precision which will make the written language a universal tool of communication. The sense of what is right and fitting will only come by practising, reading, using a good dictionary and by criticizing your own work so that you catch any false notes.

Glossary

Ablative: A term borrowed from Latin grammar to describe the case that indicates *agency*.

> They were struck *by stones*;
> he felled the tree *with an axe*;
> I had a present *from an admirer*.

Abstract noun: A noun that describes something that can be identified or recognized, but is intangible: a feeling, idea or state.

Accidence: The classification of all the variations in the forms of words in a language - the inflectional system.
see Inflection, Case.

Accusative case: *see* Objective case.

Active voice: The verb is in the active voice when the subject is the agent of the verb's action. In

> Bears eat honey,

eat is an action performed by, or relating directly to, *bears*.

Adjective: An adjective can be said to qualify or limit a noun because its application is to a particular part of the general group represented by the noun. In

> Sheep are stupid,

all sheep are insulted, but in

> Twenty sheep were grazing

the noun is limited to those sheep. Adjectives also enlarge the noun by describing attributes or characteristics:

> Girls;
> Pretty girls.

Some adjectives can be employed as abstract nouns; here *beautiful* is substituted for *beauty*:

> Search for the beautiful.

In

> The old and the wise,

the adjectives are used as concrete nouns representing people.

Adjective clause: An adjective clause qualifies a noun, its antecedent. A relative pronoun can act as a conjunction introducing the clause and must agree in person and number with the antecedent, though its case is related to its own subjective or objective position.

Adverb: An adverb modifies the meaning of the word (verb, adjective or adverb) with which it is associated. For example, we add an adverb to describe how something is done (Manner):

He played badly.

For a classification of modifications, *see* **3.78–82**.

Adverb clause: Adverb clauses behave as adverbs in a sentence. They can be classified, like adverbs, as clauses of place, reason, time, etc. *See* **3.89, 5.19**.

Agreement:

1. Singular subjects are matched with singular verbs; plural subjects need plural verbs;

   The mouse eats cheese;

   The cats eat tinned catfood.

2. Compound subjects are plural:

   Chalk and cheese are unmixable.

   The only exception is when a 3rd person pronoun joins 1st and end person pronouns in a subject; the verb then always agrees with the 1st or 2nd person, never the 3rd person:

   You and he and I ride today.

   See **4.32**

3. Collective nouns are sometimes singular, sometimes plural. *See* **3.8** (6–12).

4. Relative pronouns agree with their antecedents in number and person when they are the subject of relative clauses. *See* **5.21**.

Analysis: The analysis of a sentence is the examination, phrase by phrase, clause by clause, of its parts to see how they relate to each other. Chapter Five, **5.31–44**.

Antecedent: A noun to which a following pronoun, especially a relative pronoun, refers, as in

The *king* is in *his* counting house;

The *man who* turnips cries. . . .

Antithesis: The emphasis given to ideas by opposing similarly-phrased statements using strongly contrasted words.

The rich man's wealth is his strong city: the destruction of the poor is their poverty.

Apostrophe: A punctuation mark like the closing half of a pair of quotation marks. It shows

1. the omission of a letter: won't;

2. the possessive case of a noun: crocodile's tears.

Article: The definite article (*the*) distinguishes or emphasizes a particular thing or person. It also refers back to something mentioned previously. The indefinite article (*a* or *an*) refers to any one of a group or class rather than a particular one. It is also used to introduce or draw attention to something or someone to be discussed.

Auxiliary verb: The auxiliary verbs (*be, have, shall, will, may* and *do*) have a special part to play in forming tenses and expressing mood and voice. Some are verbs in their own right; *see* Notional words.

Brackets: *see* **6.20.**

Case: The relationship of a noun, pronoun or adjective to another word or words in a sentence and any change in form that may denote this: nominative, accusative, genitive, dative or ablative case. In English nouns are only inflected to show ownership: the possessive case, and number: plural forms. Pronouns are inflected to show the subject (nominative), object (accusative), possession (genitive) cases. The case of the indirect object (dative) is shown by prepositions – *to* or *for*, often subject to ellipsis (*see*). The case of instrument or agency (ablative) uses the prepositions *by, with* or *from*.

Case endings: *see* Inflections

Clause: A group of words which, like a sentence, has a subject and a predicate, but relates to the more important main clause. *See* Main clause, Co-ordinate clause, Dependent clause, Noun clause, Adverb clause, Adjective clause.

Collective nouns: Collective nouns, also called nouns of multitude, describe groups of people, animals or things. Some are singular, some plural; *see* **3.8** (7–12).

Colloquial speech: Language as it is spoken, using idioms, catch-phrases, abbreviations, elisions and dialect words, with regional variations in pronunciation and constructions. Colloquial English is what is used when we talk to each other without preparing or considering the way in which we speak.

Complex sentences; They have dependent clauses which are subordinate to the main clause. One complex sentence can have a number of inserted phrases and different types of dependent clauses. It may also be a compound sentence (*see*) if it has a second main clause joined to the first by a conjunction.

Compound sentence: A compound sentence consists of more than one main clause. The clauses need not be of equal importance but are always joined by a conjunction. *See* Sentence.

Conditional tenses: Although simple tenses are often used in conditional statements or clauses:

If I ran all the way, I could get there in time,

and in subjunctive *if*-clauses:

If I were a mouse, I would fight the cat,

the description 'conditional' in this book refers to a future tense with should/would:

    I would die for my beliefs.

Conjugation: The system of all the inflections and modifications of a verb which show person, number, tense, voice and mood. In English there are few inflections: the present tense (3rd person singular), the past tense, the present participle and the past participle. The other tenses are formed by adding auxiliary verbs.

Conjunction: A word that is used to connect sentences or introduce words and clauses. *See also* Conjunctive, Co-ordinating, Correlating, Disjunctive and Subordinate Conjunctions.

Conjunctive conjunctions: Conjunctions that join complete statements, expressing a positive relationship between the statements or clauses they connect.

Continuous tenses: Continuous tenses are also called 'imperfect', because the action described has not been completed; it is continuing at the present time, was continuing at some time in the past or will be continuing at some time in the future:

    I am running; I was running; I will be running.

Co-ordinate clause: A group of words forming a sentence which is joined to another sentence by a conjunction. The statement made may or may not be equal in importance to the statement made by the main clause.

Co-ordinating conjunction: A conjunction which joins together two complete statements relating in sense, or co-ordinate clauses.

Correlating conjunctions: Conjunctions that are used together because they correspond to each other. They always correlate things of the same type, that is, the same part of speech or the same sort of adverb phrase: *either – or, not only – but also*, etc.

Dative case: The case, in English, of the indirect object, expressed by using *to* or *for*, but often concealed by ellipsis.

Declension: A declension is

1. the list of a noun or pronoun's inflections (*see* Decline, Inflection);
2. the whole group of nouns that have similar case-endings.

English nouns have few inflections and are not declined.

Decline: In inflected languages, the case-endings of nouns, adjectives and pronouns are listed, or declined, in order, according to the case to which each form belongs. *See* Case, Inflection.

Defining (relative) clause: The defining relative clause states something about its antecedent that classifies or restricts the antecedent:

    1. Jumblies whose heads are blue go to sea in a sieve.

The non-defining relative clause adds parenthetic information about the antecedent without restricting it:

    2. Jumblies, whose heads are blue, go to sea in a sieve.

The clause in 1. indicates that only blue-headed Jumblies set off in sieves – sieve-going is restricted to the blue heads. The clause in 2. tells us that all Jumblies happen to have blue heads. The non-defining clause is always set off by commas to show its parenthetic application. Leave out the commas and you have a defining clause.

Dependent clause: A subordinate clause, or one whose meaning depends on the rest of the sentence.

Disjunctive conjunctions: Conjunctions that express an alternative or negative relationship between the clauses they connect: *or* and *but*.

Disjunctive pronoun: This is a French grammatical term for the pronouns that are 'disjoined' from the verb *to be*: It's *me*; It's *him*. It is also called an Emphatic Nominative and is, in English speech, a natural answer to questions of identity.

Ellipsis: The omission of words from a statement because, although their sense is needed to complete the construction, their presence is implied. The meaning is clear because the reader or hearer readily makes the right inference. It should be used with caution; ellipsis can lead to obscurity.

Emphatic Nominative: *see* Disjunctive pronoun.

Factitive verb: This is the term used to describe the verbs *calling, considering* or *making*, which have a certain type of object to complete the predicate:

    They called her Mama Bear;
    We considered him stupid;
    They made him Prime Minister.

Finite verb forms: The parts of verbs where the action is limited as far as person, number and time are concerned. In

    He kissed the babies,

the verb *kissed* is limited, or finite, because it is unchangeably singular, third person and in the past tense. *See also* Non-finite verb forms.

Future-in-the-past tense: When an action has not taken place at the time expressed in a past statement, but was, at that moment, expected to take place, we use the Future-in-the-past tense.

    I was sure that he would soon arrive.

Gender: The classification of persons, animals and objects according to their sex. Persons and animals are usually masculine or feminine; objects, except for colloquial references to one's native country, ships, cars and so on, are therefore neuter.

Genitive case: *see* Possessive case.

Gerund: A verbal noun formed by adding *-ing* to the verb stem. It can be the subject, object or complement of a sentence and also used as a simple noun or in an adverbial phrase.

Homonyms: Words that have the same spelling but different meanings:

port: a harbour   check: pattern of crossed lines

port: a wine   check: a restraint

port: a gate   check: a counterfoil

                        check: a mark

Homophones: Words that sound the same but have different meanings and are not spelled in the same way:

rain; reign; rein;

site; sight.

Imperative mood: The mood of command and exhortation. Orders,

Go home,

and instructions,

Try this one,

are given in the imperative mood.

Indicative mood: The indicative mood states facts, and asks questions. It is a factual mood.

Indirect object: An object more remote from the action of the verb than the direct object, separated from the verb by a preposition.

I shall ask you to *my party.*

Infinitive: A form of the verb that is

1. the name of the verb, i.e. *to weep;*
2. used with an auxiliary to express the meaning of the verb but does not have a subject of its own; the subject is that of the auxiliary verb;
3. used as a noun-subject or noun-object, adjective or adverb.

Inflection: An inflection (also known as an inflexion) is the change in the shape of a word to modify its meaning. The variation can show the number of persons or things involved, gender, time (in verbs), or comparison (in adjectives). In a highly inflected language the variations also indicate the relation of words to other words in sentences; the shape of a noun can show whether it is the subject, object or indirect object of the verb. It can also show possession or agency. As English has developed, it has lost most of its inflections; *see* Case, Conjugation

Intransitive verb: One that completes the action without an object; the action is not carried over but stops with the verb.

The dog barked.

In

I sat down,

down is not the object but an adverb describing how the subject sat. *See* Transitive verb.

Linguistics: The study of the nature, development and structure of language, both spoken and written, as a characteristic of human function and behaviour.

Main clause: The basic statement made by a sentence. All other clauses depend on the main clause for their meaning.

Modify: A word, usually a verb, is modified by adding an adverb to it, or qualifying it. The adverb describes the verb's action:

> he ran slowly

or qualifies an adjective:

> an unusually successful meeting.

Mood: The manner expressed by any group of verbal forms which states how the verbal forms in the group are used: whether action is simply stated as a fact, indicates a command, expresses a condition or a wish. The moods are indicative, imperative, subjunctive or optative, accordingly.

Nominative case: *see* Subjective case.

Non-defining (relative) clause: *see* Defining (relative) clause.

Non-finite verb form: Verb forms that are non-finite convey the general idea of an action without limiting it in any way.

> Running is good exercise.

The non-finite parts of the verb are the infinitive, the gerund and the participles. *See* **4.11-29.**

Notional word: One that conveys a full meaning. A noun is notional when it is used as a noun but not when it is used as an adjective. A verb is a notional verb when it is used in its own right and not as an auxiliary:

> I am happy.

Noun: A word that stands for the name of a person, thing or idea. It is also called a *substantive. Anything, nothing* and *everything* are nouns, as are *Greeks* and a *table. See* **3.6-7.**

Noun clause: A noun clause can be the subject of a sentence, or its object. When it is the object of the sentence it is preceded by *that. See* **5.17.**

Nouns of multitude: *see* Collective nouns.

Number: The number of persons or things shown by the use of a singular or plural noun, pronoun or verb form.

Object: The noun or pronoun in a sentence which is affected by, or is the recipient of, action from a transitive verb. *See also* Indirect object, Objective case.

Objective case: This case, also called the accusative case, refers to the case of a noun that is the object of a verb or, in English, follows a preposition:

> The knight rode *a charger*;
> Yankee Doodle came *to town*,
> Riding *on a pony*,
> Stuck *a feather* in his cap
> And called *it* Macaroni.

Optative mood: The optative mood expresses wish or desire with the overriding sense of uncertainty. The outcome of the wish is not determined but hangs in the balance, half-doubtful of success:

> I may be lucky;
> May it never come to pass.

Oratio obliqua: *see* Oratio recta.

Oratio recta: This is direct speech, words reproduced exactly as they were spoken, usually with quotation marks about the statement:

> She only said, 'My life is dreary';

though seldom in poetry:

> My strength is as the strength of ten
> Because my heart is pure,

when it is the poet speaking. If speech is reported indirectly, by the writer or someone else, it is oratio obliqua:

> He said his strength was as the strength of ten because his
> heart was pure.

Note the change to the past tense, which is the mark of indirect speech.

Parsing: The examination of each word in a sentence in order to determine its nature (person, number, case or tense) and its particular action or function in the sentence. Parsing is an out-of-date activity, of little use to the writer or speaker who has a sound understanding of the grammatical principles of the language.

Particles: Short unchangeable words or parts of words, particles are minor parts of speech. *A, an* and *the* are particles; so are prefixes and suffixes, and many prepositions and conjunctions. The sturdy little particles help to particularize a noun, make adverbs show direction and turn adjectives into comparatives. *See* Proclitic particles.

Parts of speech: Nouns, pronouns, verbs, adjectives, adverbs, prepositions, conjunctions and particles. For an explanation of the use of each part, see under one of these headings.

Passive voice: A verb is in the passive voice when the subject is the recipient of the verb's action:

> Honey is eaten by bears.

Honey is the subject of the sentence although the bears are doing the eating. The passive tense formation consists of the past participle with an auxiliary; *see* Active voice, Past participle.

Past continuous tense: *see* Future-in-the-past tense.

Past participle: One of the principal parts of the verb; it combines with auxiliary verbs to form tenses, acting as an adjective which describes the specific action. The action that occurs when using the past participle tells what happens to the subject; it is passive. *See* **4.22-3.**

Past tense: The past tense is a principal part of the verb, describing actions and states that are in the past or have already taken place. It is a finite verb-form:

> I walked; it rained.

Perfect tense: The perfect tense refers to completed action, whether it took place in the past, has taken place at the present time or is to be completed at a known time in the future:

> I had been to the theatre;
> I have taken the exam;
> They will have arrived before we leave.

See also Simple tenses.

Person: A pronoun or verb is said to be in the first person when it refers to the person speaking: *I am hungry*; in the second person when it refers to the person spoken to: *You are eating*; and it is in the third person when it refers to the person or thing spoken about: *He is washing* the plates; *It has been eaten.*

Personal pronoun: The pronoun that is substituted for the name of, or the word naming, a pronoun: I, you, he, she, it we, you, they.

Phrase: A group of words which relate to the meaning of the whole sentence but which do not include a finite verb:

> Longing to taste it, she. . . .

Pluperfect tenses: The pluperfect tenses refer to an action finished or completed at a moment in the past:

> I had closed the window before the rain fell.

Plural: The form of a noun, pronoun or verb which denotes more than one person or thing referred to:

> foot – singular; feet – plural.

See Singular.

Possessive case: The form of a noun or pronoun that shows ownership or possession, also called the genitive case:

> The man's hat;
> Her dog.

Predicate: The predicate asserts something about the subject of a

sentence: what the subject does or what happens to the subject.
It always contains a verb, expressing the subject's action or state,
which can be an intransitive verb:

I *sneezed*,

or a transitive verb carrying the action to an object:

The cook *makes porridge.*

The object can be qualified by an adjective:

The cook *makes lumpy porridge,*

and the action of the verb can be modified by an adverb:

The cook *makes lumpy porridge quickly.*

The predicate includes dependent or subordinate clauses with the
effect of adjectives or adverbs:

The cook *makes lumpy porridge, which no one will eat, because
she is always in a hurry.*

It does not include noun clauses that are the subject of the sentence or
adjective clauses that qualify the subject.

Prefix: A group of letters attached to the beginning of a word to alter
its meaning, indicating, among other things, recurrence (re-), negation
(non- and un-), opposition (anti-) and singularity (mono-). *See also*
Particles.

Preposition: A word that shows

1. the case of a word in a sentence;
2. the relationship of words in an adjective phrase:

A man *of honour* – an honourable man;

3. the relationship of words in an adverb phrase:

He wrote *in haste* – he wrote hastily;

4. position, direction, time, manner, etc.

See **5.1–6.**

Present participle: One of the principal parts of the verb, it describes
the specific action indicated by the auxiliary verb with which it forms
a tense. The present participle is active because it represents something
done or performed by the subject.

Present tense: The present tense, also one of the principal parts of
the verb, describes actions which are going on at the moment of speaking: I *walk*; it *rains*. It is one of the finite verb forms.

Proclitic particle: A proclitic particle, or proclitic, is a monosyllable
'loosely attached' to the following word, having a strengthening
effect: (to)wards; (in)to; (un)necessary, etc. *See also* Particles.

Pronoun: A pronoun is a word whose first duty is to stand in for a
noun. It can

1. avoid repetition of a previously mentioned or indicated noun;

Mary is going to Ascot; *she* enjoys race meetings.
2. act less definitely in standing in for a noun that has not been specifically indicated:
I'd like to know *who* broke the window;
3. act as an adjective in describing possession or pointing something out;
her car; *those* cabbages;
4. act as a conjunction introducing a relative clause.
See Conjunction, Relative clause and **3.25-72.**
Proper noun: A noun that identifies an individual person, place or named object.
Qualify: To express some quality belonging to a noun, so limiting the noun:
She has *big* feet.
Qualification is also the effect that an adverb has on a verb when it modifies the verb. *See* Adverb, Modify.
Relative clause: A clause introduced by a relative pronoun that describes something in the main clause as an adjective would:
The man *who robbed the bank* has been arrested;
or as an adverb would:
I walk past the stone *where witches meet.*
See Defining clauses.
Sentence: There are three types of sentences. Each type can be rearranged to present information in a different order, or to make material more interesting to read.
1. Simple sentence:
Harold grumbles;
Roast lamb was eaten by Mary.
2. Compound sentence: This is in two parts, each with a subject and predicate; the parts are joined by a conjunction and each part is a co-ordinate clause.
It was an Abyssinian maid,
And on her dulcimer she played,
Singing of Mount Abora.
3. Complex sentence: This contains dependent or subordinate clauses which enlarge the main statement.
Although I attach no sort of credit to the fantastic Indian legend of the gem, I must acknowledge, before I conclude, that I am influenced by a certain superstition of my own in this matter.
Sequence of tenses: Tenses in the subordinate clauses of a sentence

must relate to the same general time-period as that in the main clause. For the exception, *see* Universal statement. *See also* **4.35.**

Simple tenses: They describe actions that are complete, will be complete or were complete at the time stated. The exception is the Simple Present, often called 'Indefinite'. *I wait for the bus* may become *I will be waiting for the bus* if the bus has not arrived as the statement ends. The word 'simple' has been used in **4.34** to describe the parts of tenses that make straightforward statements, to distinguish them from continuous (*see*) and conditional (*see*) forms and to avoid the confusion caused by the names of the Perfect and Pluperfect tenses, a confusion inappropriate in a reference book.

Singular: The form of a noun, pronoun or verb that denotes a single person or thing.

Subject: The subject is the point of origin of a sentence. Without it there would be nothing about which a predication could be made. It is the person, thing or idea that engenders the thought; it can be a single noun or several, but it or they must always be in the nominative or subjective case:

> They; oatmeal; The Forged Steel Valve Company.

It can be a noun identified by a qualification:

> The lively horse; Able Seaman Charlie, the cat.

The subject can be plural and can include two or more nouns:

> Rosicrucians;
> Lazy cats and dirty dogs
> Are shunned by upright sober hogs.

Subjective case: Also called the nominative case, it is the case of the subject, the prime mover of the verb. Even when the subject is not expressed, as in the imperative mood, its invisible presence is still in the subjective case.

Subjunctive mood: The mood of actions or states that are conceived, desired or imagined and not (or not yet) fact. It deals with hypothetical events, suppositions and desires. *See* **4.40-4.**

Subordinate clause: A subordinate clause is a group of words that takes the place of a single noun, adjective or adverb. A noun clause can be the subject or object of a sentence. Adjective and adverb clauses qualify or modify a word or words in the main clause.

Subordinating conjunctions: Conjunctions which introduce or join subordinate clauses to main clauses in complex sentences, or to other subordinate clauses. *See* **5.16-20.**

Substantive: A grammatical term for a noun. *See* Noun.

Suffix: A group of letters attached to the end of a word to add to its meaning: *-ion* (intention); *-ly* (suddenly); *-er* (brighter). *See* Particles, Proclitic particles.

Synonyms: Words whose meanings are very close and which can, in the right circumstances, be substituted for one another: *easy – facile.* The context should always govern the choice. There are very few true synonyms – words whose meanings coincide exactly. MEU gives only one example: *furze* and *gorse.*

Syntax: To express ideas, words are grouped together. The study of the relationship between the grouped words when they form sentences is syntax.

Tense: A means of expressing, through the form of the verb or auxiliary verb, the time at which action takes place, has taken place or will take place. It also distinguishes the action which is completed from action which is continuing.

Terminology: The terms used within a particular art or science to describe special things, events or occurrences.

Transition: The linking of subject to object by passing over the action from one to the other through a transitive verb.

Transitive verb: One that must carry the action or assertion over to an object to complete its meaning:

Martha *made* marmalade.

Universal statement: A statement that carries or contains a permanent or immutable truth without any limitation of time. It is therefore made in the present tense. If the main clause of a sentence is in the past but a dependent relative clause contains a universal statement, the tense of the statement need not agree with that in the main clause.

He told me that justice is impartial.

Verb: Without a verb, a group of words is not a sentence. The verb is the word that declares something or makes an assertion about the noun or noun-equivalent that is the subject. It can declare action,

The dish ran away with the spoon;

or state,

All is calm.

See Intransitive verb, Transitive verb.

Voice: The way in which the verb form is changed to show how the subject is related to the action. *See* Active voice, Passive voice.

Index

A paragraph number in bold type after an entry refers to the main discussion of the topic; roman type indicates that it is mentioned in the numbered paragraph; numbers after sub-entries show that it is mentioned in relation to another entry.